Classics

KILMARNOCK

FOOTBALL CLUB

Classics

KILMARNOCK
FOOTBALL CLUB

GORDON ALLISON

TEMPUS

Front cover: Paul Wright turns away having just netted the only goal of the 1997 Scottish Cup Final. Jim McIntyre and Dylan Kerr rush to congratulate him.

First published 2004

Tempus Publishing Limited
The Mill, Brimscombe Port,
Stroud, Gloucestershire, GL5 2QG

British Library Cataloguing in Publication Data.
A catalogue record for this book is available from the British Library.

ISBN 0 7524 3188 9

Typesetting and origination by Tempus Publishing Limited
Printed in Great Britain by Midway Colour Print, Wiltshire.

Acknowledgements

I wish to thank the following individuals and organizations for their help with this publication: Richard Cairns, Sandy Ferguson, Colin MacMillan, Ross McKenzie, Jackie McInally, Alex Milligan, James Rowan, the staff of the reference library in the Dick Institute in Kilmarnock and the staff of Glasgow's Mitchell Library, *The Daily Record*, the *Kilmarnock Standard*, the Colour Copy Centre in Irvine and last, but certainly not least, Mrs Anne Allison. My sincere apologies in advance to anyone I have forgotten to include.

Introduction

Fifty classic matches. Well, that should be no problem, or so I thought. I would just sit down and select my fifty matches one evening and then take it from there. What a misconception! Six months later I had still not fully decided the games to be included.

What is the definition of a classic match? Well, obviously you must include all our cup final appearances. But do you really want to recall the heartbreakers where we ended up with the second prize? Perhaps if we had played well and been unlucky then they could be included, or perhaps not. High-scoring games? Well yes, but only if we were on the right side of the trouncing! Promotion, relegation and championship deciders, special games involving the opening of a new stadium or new floodlights, a particularly significant debut, high-scoring draws, shock results... I deliberated for months, first including and then deleting games from the final selection, eventually being forced to choose with deadline day fast approaching.

So inside this humble offering you will *not* be able to read of classic Kilmarnock matches such as the first-ever Scottish Cup tie, played on 18 October 1873 and so well-organised that Killie played the entire match with ten players and to this day it remains in doubt whether the result was 2-0 or 3-0 to Renton. Similarly excluded is one of the first football matches played under electric lights, as far back as 8 November 1878. It was against the local rivals of the time, Kilmarnock Portland. So great a success was this enterprise that it was to be seventy-five years before Kilmarnock Football Club played another home match under lights (this one was against Manchester United on 28 October 1953) and it is not included either! What is offered within these pages is my choice of matches and mine alone. My main regret would be that I witnessed only seventeen of the matches first-hand. I hope you enjoy reading this book, and if you are a Killie fan I apologise in advance if one of your favourite games is not one of my fifty classic matches.

Classic Matches

5 April 1884	Kilmarnock *v.* Hurlford	Ayrshire Cup Final Replay
21 February 1891	Kilmarnock *v.* Hurlford	Ayrshire Cup Final
24 August 1895	Kilmarnock *v.* Motherwell	Scottish League Division Two
5 December 1896	Kilmarnock *v.* Motherwell	Scottish Qualifying Cup Final
26 March 1898	Kilmarnock *v.* Rangers	Scottish Cup Final
19 August 1899	St Mirren *v.* Kilmarnock	Scottish League Division One
26 August 1899	Kilmarnock *v.* Celtic	Scottish League Division One
15 December 1900	Queens Park *v.* Kilmarnock	Scottish League Division One
4 January 1908	Port Glasgow Athletic *v.* Kilmarnock	Scottish League Division One
21 April 1917	Celtic *v.* Kilmarnock	Scottish League Division One
17 April 1920	Kilmarnock *v.* Albion Rovers	Scottish Cup Final
23 March 1929	Kilmarnock *v.* Celtic	Scottish Cup Semi-Final
6 April 1929	Kilmarnock *v.* Rangers	Scottish Cup Final
18 February 1933	Kilmarnock *v.* Rangers	Scottish Cup Third Round
23 September 1933	Kilmarnock *v.* Airdrie	Scottish League Division One
2 January 1936	Kilmarnock *v.* Ayr United	Scottish League Division One
5 March 1938	Celtic *v.* Kilmarnock	Scottish Cup Third Round
23 March 1938	Ayr United *v.* Kilmarnock	Scottish Cup Quarter-Final Replay
2 April 1938	Rangers *v.* Kilmarnock	Scottish Cup Semi-Final
14 January 1950	Queens Park *v.* Kilmarnock	Scottish League B Division
4 October 1952	Rangers *v.* Kilmarnock	League Cup Semi-Final
27 March 1957	Celtic *v.* Kilmarnock	Scottish Cup Semi-Final Replay
9 November 1957	Rangers *v.* Kilmarnock	Scottish League Division One
27 February 1960	Kilmarnock *v.* Motherwell	Scottish Cup Third Round

1 June 1960	Kilmarnock *v.* Burnley	New York International Soccer League Tournament
26 November 1960	Rangers *v.* Kilmarnock	Scottish League Division One
29 September 1962	Kilmarnock *v.* Airdrie	Scottish League Division One
10 October 1962	Rangers *v.* Kilmarnock	League Cup Semi-Final
27 March 1963	Kilmarnock *v.* Celtic	Scottish League Division One
8 February 1964	Kilmarnock *v.* Falkirk	Scottish League Division One
22 September 1964	Kilmarnock *v.* Eintracht Frankfurt	Fairs Cities Cup First Round, Second Leg
28 October 1964	Kilmarnock *v.* Celtic	Scottish League Division One
24 April 1965	Hearts *v.* Kilmarnock	Scottish League Division One
17 November 1965	Kilmarnock *v.* Real Madrid	European Cup First Round, First Leg
2 November 1966	Kilmarnock *v.* Royal Antwerp	Fairs Cities Cup Second Round, Second Leg
11 February 1967	Kilmarnock *v.* Rangers	Scottish League Division One
19 May 1967	Leeds United *v.* Kilmarnock	Fairs Cities Cup Semi-Final, First Leg
21 September 1968	Rangers *v.* Kilmarnock	Scottish League Division One
26 October 1968	Kilmarnock *v.* Raith Rovers	Scottish League Division One
4 January 1969	Kilmarnock *v.* Rangers	Scottish League Division One
30 October 1976	Kilmarnock *v.* Ayr United	Scottish League Premier Division
6 March 1978	Kilmarnock *v.* Celtic	Scottish Cup Fourth Round Replay
5 August 1979	Rangers *v.* Kilmarnock	Tennent-Caledonian Cup Final
13 May 1989	Queen of the South *v.* Kilmarnock	Scottish League First Division
28 August 1993	Rangers *v.* Kilmarnock	Scottish Premier League
7 May 1994	Kilmarnock *v.* Rangers	Scottish Premier League
24 May 1997	Kilmarnock *v.* Falkirk	Tennents Scottish Cup Final
17 April 1999	Dunfermline *v.* Kilmarnock	Scottish League Premier Division
28 October 2000	Rangers *v.* Kilmarnock	Scottish League Premier Division
6 February 2001	St Mirren *v.* Kilmarnock	CIS Insurance League Cup Semi-Final

A team group from 1886. President Dan Gilmour sits proudly with the Kilmarnock Charity Cup in front of him, after defeating Ayr 5-0.

The players who finally ended Kilmarnock's seven-year exile in 'B' Division of the Scottish League in 1954. From left to right, back row: R. Collins, J. Hood, J. Brown, J. Russell, R. Thyne, J. Middlemass. Front row: M. Murray, W. Harvey, W. Jack, D. Curlett, T. Heneaghan.

Killie number nine Bobby Williamson has just tapped in the injury-time winner in the 2-1 victory at Ibrox in August 1993 and the fans behind the goal go berserk.

Mr James Moffat, the perfect gentleman to whom Kilmarnock Football Club owes so very much, with Mrs Moffat and the Scottish Cup.

KILMARNOCK v. HURLFORD

Date: 5 April 1884 **Match title:** Ayrshire Cup Final Replay
Location: Holm Quarry, Kilmarnock

Kilmarnock Football Club became, in the late 1860s, the first club to be formed in Ayrshire. The early matches were exclusively friendlies, and the club's first taste of competitive football did not come until the inauguration of the Scottish Cup in 1873. Over the next few years various local competitions were initiated in Ayrshire, many of them for charitable purposes. The Ayrshire Cup appeared in 1877, the Kilmarnock Charity Cup in 1881 and the Ayr Charity Cup soon after. Despite being the 'parent' club in the county, Kilmarnock found that others who perhaps took the game more seriously were achieving greater success when it came to winning trophies. Names like Mauchline (the first-ever winners of the Ayrshire Cup), Kilmarnock Athletic, Lugar and Kilmarnock Portland were being engraved on cups and Kilmarnock's name was not.

However, in season 1883/84 the club reached the Ayrshire Cup final after disposing of Portland, who actually withdrew from their first-round meeting and folded completely for financial reasons, Maybole by 4 goals to 3, Lugar Boswell 3-2 and bitter rivals Kilmarnock Athletic 3-1 on Athletic's own ground, Holm Quarry. As was often the practice in those days the team losing a cup tie would find some spurious grounds to lodge a protest and seek a replay, and such was certainly the case in 1883/84 as Killie survived protests from Maybole, Lugar and Athletic in turn!

On 22 March 1884 Kilmarnock met Hurlford at Holm Quarry in the Ayrshire Cup final. Killie had in fact reached the final previously in 1882, but lost to Portland on that occasion. The 1884 final was drawn 2-2 and a replay set for the same venue on 5 April.

It should be stated that in those days the Ayrshire Cup was considered a very serious affair and the prestige involved was considerable. Most of the towns and even many small villages in Ayrshire entered the competition and local rivalries were intense. Special trains were laid on to bring fans from all over the county into Kilmarnock for the final. Many an Ayrshire Cup tie ended in mayhem and would invariably be followed by letters to the editor of the local paper as claims and counterclaims of foul deeds and underhand tactics being used by opponents were made, while naturally the writer would insist that his own team were paragons of virtue and badly mistreated. This could generally be taken as an indication that his side had lost. Ayrshire Cup ties in 1884 were no place for the faint-hearted.

The interest manifested by those present at Holm Quarry on 5 April for the replay was intense. An extremely strong wind was blowing towards the pavilion end as Walker of Kilmarnock kicked off playing against it. Almost at once Killie's ace forward Alex Higgins (soon to be capped by Scotland) set off on one of his characteristic solo runs and was not halted until he was almost within shooting distance. Hurlford then took the initiative, but whenever one of their forwards threatened to shoot he was immediately surrounded by Killie defenders and crowded out. When the ball did get near goalkeeper McCall, the Hurlford forwards rushed in heedless of the consequences and men were soon rolling on top of each other. Play was getting a bit rough. Then 'San' Goudie, one of three Goudies in the Hurlford team, found a space, and, holding off a challenge from Killie's George Black, steadied himself and from a fair distance shot his side into the lead.

Kilmarnock 2
Wark
Higgins

Hurlford 1
A. Goudie

Gradually Killie fought their way back into the game against the strong wind and won a corner kick on the right. It was played across to the back post where 'Jebb' Wark was waiting to send a neat header past Bowman to make it 1-1. Killie pressed ahead as the game turned in their favour and just before half-time Higgins netted to give them a 2-1 lead.

The consensus of opinion at half-time was that the match was virtually over, with Killie now ahead and having the advantage of the powerful wind in the second half. Against this wind Hurlford managed to keep possession well, but rarely came close to scoring, while Killie seemed content to hold on and play a safe and steady game, keeping Hurlford in check. Wright, Hurlford's best player, strove manfully to get his side back on level terms, but to no avail, as Kilmarnock comfortably held on for a 2-1 victory and the club's first trophy. Some idea of the strength of the wind during the game can be gauged by reference to the following statistics:

First half:	Hurlford goal kicks: 1	Corners: 5
	Kilmarnock goal kicks: 17	Corners: 2
Second half:	Hurlford goal kicks: 28	Corners: 0
	Kilmarnock goal kicks: 1	Corners: 5

Almost inevitably Hurlford lodged a protest relating to the eligibility of Killie players Higgins, Plumtree and McCall. The latter, they held, was ineligible owing to the fact that he was now resident in Glasgow. The Ayrshire Football Association held a meeting the following Wednesday that led to the presentation of the cup and badges being postponed. However, when they met to consider the case, a majority declared in favour of Kilmarnock and the presentation took place in the Crown Inn Hall on the evening of Monday 21 April. Kilmarnock FC had its first trophy and obviously enjoyed the feeling, as the Ayrshire Cup was retained in 1885 and 1886.

The magnificent Ayrshire Cup: solid silver, standing 30ins high and made by John Cameron & Son of Kilmarnock. It cost well in excess of £100 in 1877.

Kilmarnock: McCall, Plumtree, Young, Grier, Burnett, A. Black, G. Black, Higgins, Walker, Wark, Wallace.

Hurlford: Bowman, Banks, R. Goudie, Wright, Fulton, H. Smith, Black, A. Goudie, Ross, J. Smith, T. Goudie.

KILMARNOCK v. HURLFORD

Date: 21 February 1891   **Match title:** Ayrshire Cup Final
Location: Holm Quarry, Kilmarnock

After the breakthrough that saw Kilmarnock lift their first trophy in the 1884 Ayrshire Cup final, further successes soon followed. Apart from the retaining of this cup in 1885 and 1886, the Kilmarnock Charity Cup was won in May of 1884 and again in May 1886, as well as the Ayr Charity Cup, which was won resoundingly 5-1 at Beresford Park against Ayr on 31 March 1888, this being the first time this cup had ever left Ayr. However, by 1891 most of the players who had formed the backbone of these winning sides had departed and it was now a much different and much younger team that represented the club. A disappointing defeat in a replay against Annbank in the Scottish Cup gave extra impetus to Killie's efforts to regain the still-prized Ayrshire Cup. Victories over Irvine (5-0), Lanemark (15-0), Kilbirnie (3-1 after a 1-1 draw) and Kilmarnock Athletic (3-2) got Killie into the final, where they would compete against Hurlford once more for what was considered to be the finest and probably the most expensively produced football trophy in the country.

Hurlford at that time had a much more experienced team and were most people's favourites to win. As a guide to recent form, much was being made of the fact that just seven days before the final Hurlford had beaten Kilmarnock Athletic 6-0 on Athletic's own ground, whereas Kilmarnock had only beaten Athletic 3-2 in the cup semi-final a week before that.

In fine weather, a record crowd for Ayrshire turned up at Holm Quarry, thousands arriving by train. Some among the throng were offering odds of ten to one against a Killie victory. How wrong could they be?

Andrew Kelvin opened the scoring for Kilmarnock and by half-time the odds had been shown to be utterly ridiculous as the Killie players retired to their dressing room three goals ahead. Their supporters' enthusiasm knew no bounds; Hurlford's defenders could not get anywhere near the quick, sharp and intelligent manoeuvres of the Kilmarnock forwards. Hurlford came out more determined at the start of the second half and for fifteen minutes were on top, but could not convert pressure into goals and were on several occasions thwarted by the brilliance of 'keeper James McIlroy. Unfortunately for Hurlford, Kilmarnock soon regained the supremacy they had shown in the first half, and while McIlroy shone for his side, his opposite number in goal for Hurlford, Cowan, brought up specially from the Isle of Wight, proved a huge disappointment and was blamed for several of the goals. The goals came at regular intervals, only halting when the score reached 7-1. This game was to be a personal triumph for left-winger Andrew Kelvin (later to play for Liverpool), who hit no less than five of the goals, the other two coming from Robert Tannahill and Bobby Orr. Tannahill also later played for various clubs in England, including Bolton in the 1894 FA Cup final. Contemporary reporters described Kelvin's performance as 'sublime' and he was the main architect of the victory by what was reckoned to be the youngest team ever to win the Ayrshire Cup. Incidentally, Kelvin's grandson of the same name later played for Kilmarnock in the 1930s.

A clear factor in the victory had been the superior fitness of the Killie players. For this the credit could be given to the legendary trainer J.Q. McPherson, yet another who later found his way into English football, taking up the trainer's post with

Kilmarnock 7	Hurlford 1
Kelvin (5)	*Unknown*
Tannahill	
Orr	

The team that beat Hurlford 7-1 in the Ayrshire Cup final of 1891.

Newcastle United which he held for many years. He also had the unique experience of being trainer to both the Scottish and English national teams, although not at the same time!

Probably the main factor behind this surprisingly comprehensive victory had been overconfidence on the part of the more experienced Hurlford players. So confident were they that they attacked recklessly at all times and gave little thought to defending, and this cost them dearly. This victory meant that Killie had gone through the competition scoring 34 goals and conceding only 5. It should also be noted that four members of this Kilmarnock side won full international caps for Scotland, namely James Orr, James 'Bummer' Campbell, Jocky Johnstone and David McPherson. The Hurlford officials let it be known that they were extremely unhappy with the performance not only of the unfortunate Cowan but also of several others who were felt to have let the side down. Even the Kilmarnock players had not expected to triumph over one of their main rivals by such a margin, but truly this match belonged to one man in particular – Andrew Kelvin.

Kilmarnock: McIlroy, Hunter, J. Orr, Paterson, Campbell, Johnstone, Tannahill, D. McPherson, R. Orr, Andrew, Kelvin.

Hurlford: Cowan, Wright, W. Dunlop, Hamilton, Smith, McDill, King, J. Morgan, J. Irvine, Morgan, Ritchie.

KILMARNOCK v. MOTHERWELL

Date: 24 August 1895
Location: Rugby Park

Match title: Scottish League Division Two

By 1895 it was clearly evident that Kilmarnock had outgrown parochial Ayrshire football, where they were becoming totally dominant and much too strong for the local opposition, so as a consequence the club applied for election to the Scottish League. At the Annual Meeting of the League in June 1895, Kilmarnock and Linthouse were elected to replace Cowlairs and Dundee Wanderers in Division Two of the League. Excitement closely followed by disappointment was the order of the day on Saturday 17 August 1895 when Killie lost their first-ever League match 3-1 against Leith Athletic in Edinburgh and generally gave a below-par performance, much to the disenchantment of their supporters, albeit only temporarily. The following week saw Killie play their first-ever home League match and Lanarkshire rivals Motherwell were the opposition. Prior to this game much discussion took place with regard to the potential attendance, given that admission would now be sixpence for an adult, whereas before joining the League it had always been only threepence. In the event the size of the crowd, at a little over 2,000, was deemed to be quite satisfactory by all concerned.

At four o'clock on a lovely day, Killie kicked off League football at Rugby Park showing only one change from the previous Saturday, Rab Brown replacing Tom Busby at full-back. In the early stages play was pretty even, but after thirty minutes, just as it seemed that Kilmarnock were getting on top, it was Motherwell who opened the scoring. The 'Well strongman Harry Gray broke away and passed to Lynch, who scored a beauty. Far from being a decisive lead it was a false dawn for the visitors, as from that point onward Motherwell were hardly ever in the game. Five minutes after the opener Killie equalised, Watson getting the final touch after a scrimmage took place in front of the Motherwell goalmouth. (For those unfamiliar with the word 'scrimmage' it was originally a nineteenth-century term for what today we would call a goalmouth scramble, only worse. The word forms the root of the current term 'scrum' as still used in both codes of rugby.) Just a few minutes later Richie McAvoy drove in a second and the home crowd roared their delight. Killie pressed from there on in until half-time, and it was generally thought that now that they would be attacking the dressing-room end, which was always their preference, all hope for Motherwell was lost. Such was the firm belief of the Killie support at that time!

The second half was all one way with Kilmarnock totally dominating, apart from the award of a penalty kick to the visitors midway through this half, but even this was missed, with James 'General' Gordon bringing off a fine save (students of history will spot that the nickname was a tribute to the heroic but deceased General Gordon of Khartoum fame). Motherwell just could not cope with the tiny Killie forwards William Fisher, David Watson and Richard Cox, looking clumsy by comparison, and with Davie McPherson completely controlling the midfield further goals were inevitable. Cox got in to score a third for Killie and 'Well then simply collapsed, with two further goals from Cox, to give him a hat-trick, and another two shared by McPherson and Fisher taking the final score to 7-1. After their poor performance in the first League game, doubts had arisen over the ability of the

---

Kilmarnock 7
Watson, McAvoy
Cox (3), McPherson
Fisher

Motherwell 1
Lynch

Left: Tom Busby. A tough-tackling full-back who served Killie well from 1894 to 1903. *Middle:* Robert 'Baker' Brown. Kilmarnock-born Rab served Killie as a defender from 1892 to 1901, and remained a loyal supporter of the club until his death in December 1950. *Right:* John 'Jocky' Johnstone. Little Jocky, a Scotland international, was a marvellous half-back with the club from 1889 to 1901.

Kilmarnock team to cope with the step up in class to League football, with particular worries about the defence. The doubters were soon silenced as, following this thrashing of Motherwell, just one week later Killie beat Morton 5-1. Clearly Division Two football would not be above them after all.

A 7-1 victory in a game conducted in the fairest possible manner, with outplayed 'Well never resorting to foul play, was certainly an excellent way to celebrate the first-ever home League match! On a sadder note, Killie's full-back in this match, Peter Maxwell, died less than three months later on Friday 15 November from typhoid fever, aged only twenty-two. Kilmarnock finished that first League season in a respectable fourth position, Motherwell finished eighth.

Kilmarnock: Gordon, R. Brown, Maxwell, McPherson, J. Brown, Johnstone, Watson, Fisher, Campbell, McAvoy, Cox.
Motherwell: Haddow, Collins, Daly, Hodge, Steel, Thomas, Lynch, Goldie, Gray, Edgar, Galloway.

KILMARNOCK v. MOTHERWELL

Date: 5 December 1896   **Match title:** Scottish Qualifying Cup Final
Location: Hampden Park

Kilmarnock Football Club had thoroughly established itself as the major club in Ayrshire, and it was time to move on and become established on a national level. As already mentioned in the previous match report, in the summer of 1895 the club had applied for and been granted a place in Scottish League Division Two. Nevertheless, they were still required by virtue of League status to qualify for the Scottish Cup proper, and this meant going into the Scottish Qualifying Cup competition, where they would go into a draw along with various other clubs, many of whom could only be classed as 'minnows'. Only those teams reaching the later stages were then allowed into the Scottish Cup itself. This was actually only the second season the Qualifying Cup had been a competition in its own right. Killie certainly rattled in the goals in a storming run to the final of the competition; beaten en route were Lugar Boswell 6-2, Saltcoats Victoria 13-2, Ayr 7-1, Hurlford 4-2, Partick Thistle 5-2 and Dunblane 2-0. Kilmarnock's opponents in the final were Motherwell.

Prior to the final, doubts were raised as to the wisdom of using Hampden Park for this game, as the attendance, given that no Glasgow clubs were involved, might be pretty low, especially as Third Lanark were playing Celtic at the same time in a League match just down the road at Cathkin.

These fears seemed to have some foundation when, at two o'clock, the ground was still almost empty, but then the trains from Kilmarnock and Motherwell rolled in and Hampden quickly filled up. The pitch was like a bowling green, although the ground itself was a little slippery, as Kilmarnock entered the field first in their blue and white stripes, followed shortly after by the 'Well in a gaudy light blue. Killie kicked off and almost immediately Richmond and Campbell combined to create a dangerous situation. Inside three minutes ex-Killie 'keeper Gordon was forced to make a save, which he managed, but he looked unsure. Killie seemed to have much better teamwork and attacked again through little winger Watson, who could not be contained as he went down the right wing and crossed to young Robert Richmond, who wasted no time in sticking the ball in the net. Motherwell hit back, Ostler shooting over the bar after he had made a break from the halfway line. Ostler and Edgar seemed to be the main men on the 'Well side. Ostler in particular, with his ginger-haired cranium, seemed to be all over the pitch. A scrimmage took place in front of the Killie goal but was ultimately cleared up and Killie fans breathed again. Returning to the other end, Richmond and Campbell missed chances and the Ayrshire fans winced. They were to wince a bit more minutes later as Edgar, in possession twenty-five yards out, steadied himself and struck a fine shot at goal. Ralston seemed to have it, but it eluded him and rolled into the net. Twenty minutes played and it was 1-1. From this point until half-time play went from end to end, but latterly Killie had begun to establish superiority and looked more likely to score, however when the teams left the field at the interval it was still all square. Killie's legendary centre forward 'Bummer' Campbell was being well policed by the formidable Ostler, with neither player holding anything back, but always in good spirit. The game was still in the balance, but this was about to change and it was Kilmarnock who would take charge of the second half. After immense pressure, winger Alex McLean, who had not had one of his better games,

---

Kilmarnock 4   **Motherwell 1**
Richmond, Campbell   *Edgar*
McAvoy, McPherson

The Qualifying Cup winners. From left to right, back row: J.Q. .McPherson (Trainer), T. Busby, A. Alexander (Treasurer), J. Ralston, J. Taylor (Secretary), R. Brown, R. Thomson (Vice-President). Middle row: D. Watson, C. Smith, J. Campbell, J.W. Somerville (Vice-President), R. Richmond, A. McLean, R. Gibson. Front row: D. McPherson, A. Paterson, J. Johnstone.

knocked the ball forward to Campbell, who drove it into the net through the legs of several defenders. Motherwell never really recovered from this blow and, with their fans roaring them on, Killie launched another raid. A scrimmage ensued which was ended when McAvoy emerged to give the ball its final touch over the line. Motherwell were now struggling and McPherson then struck a beauty which flew into the net off the inside of the post. It was now 4-1 and three goals had been scored by Killie in the final twenty minutes of the game. Great jubilation greeted the final whistle; Kilmarnock had taken another step forward by winning a national competition for the first time. It had also been a clean and sporting contest and it was agreed by all that the officials Mr McLeod, Mr Robertson and Mr Sellars had done extremely well. A large crowd met the returning team at Kilmarnock Railway Station and a horse-drawn carriage took them down the street accompanied by loud cheering. The cup was put on view in Messrs Cameron & Sons, Jewellers, Kilmarnock.

As a postscript it should be noted that the game attracted the biggest gate in Glasgow that Saturday. £100 and 5 shillings was taken, £10 more than was drawn at the Third Lanark *v.* Celtic match and also more than at the Rangers *v.* Clyde encounter.

Kilmarnock: Ralston, Busby, R. Brown, D. McPherson, Paterson, Johnstone, Watson, McAvoy, Campbell, Richmond, McLean.
Motherwell: Gordon, Stewart, Neil, Thomas, Ostler, Daly, Galloway, Edgar, Maxwell, Goldie, Watson.

KILMARNOCK v. RANGERS

Date: 26 March 1898   **Match title:** Scottish Cup Final
Location: Hampden Park

The steady progress made by Kilmarnock over the last few years was maintained in season 1897/98. In only their third season in the League the club comfortably took the Division Two championship, but of even greater significance was their appearance in the Scottish Cup final. Reaching the final was particularly satisfying given Killie's controversial loss to Dumbarton in the semi-final in 1897.

On the day of the final, queues had been forming from ten o'clock in the morning out into the street and around the railway station as fans waited patiently to be transported in both special and ordinary trains to the big city. The town had never seen anything like it before. The morning began brightly, but later snowflakes started to fall and it turned into a very cold day. Kilmarnock were by no means favourites to win the cup, as the opposition was the powerful Glasgow Rangers, but that did not deter the fans who left in confident mood.

Killie took to the field first and the cheers that met them exceeded in volume those that were to greet Rangers when they followed. Killie's McPherson won the toss and wisely elected to take wind advantage in the first half. Rangers kicked off, but in the early stages made little impact on the Kilmarnock defence. A Jocky Johnstone pass to Rab Findlay led to Killie's first attack, but Findlay shot wide under pressure from Nick Smith. Shortly after Alex Smith headed the ball into the Killie net, but the referee had already blown to stop play for a foul committed by Brown on Miller. Kilmarnock returned to the Rangers end, Findlay crossed to Muir, who for once failed to make good use it but did much better just a minute later when a stinging shot brought out a fine save from Dickie. This was the prelude to an onslaught on the Rangers' goal, and sustained pressure was eased only when McPherson got up to shoot over the Killie bar. Bobby Muir was giving a fine display of his dribbling skills, eluding defenders and sending in crosses that caused alarm to Dickie and his defenders. Johnstone then sent in a rocket shot that Dickie could not hold, but managed to stop before it crossed the line. A series of corner kicks taken by Findlay followed, but a goal for the Rugby Parkers, which would have been fully merited, just would not come. Rangers and their fans now realised just how much they had underestimated their opponents. The game was not being contested in the best possible spirit; apparently this was partly caused by the chagrin of some Rangers players, notably Gibson and Hyslop, who had not bargained for meeting such stiff opposition and more than once both resorted to tactics which many in the crowd had thought them incapable of practising. Rangers were finding it hard to get back into the game; when they did attack, the Kilmarnock defenders showed such determination that Rangers could make little progress. Towards half-time Rangers did succeed in imposing themselves, but despite the best efforts of Hamilton, Miller and Alex Smith, they had just as much success as Killie when it came to converting chances into goals. The teams went in at half-time at 0-0, but Kilmarnock really should have had a lead on the overall play. Now they would face the breeze in the second half.

Rangers were first back on the attack, but Alex Smith's powerful shot found McAllan equal to it. Killie's Findlay and Reid combined well to create an opening,

Rangers 2	Kilmarnock 0
A. Smith	
Hamilton	

but Muir shot Findlay's pass over the top. The stalemate was broken midway through the second half. Miller and Hyslop had by now changed places, but it was Hamilton who burst away on the right, dodged Brown and sent the ball across to Ayrshire-born Alex Smith at the back post. He steadied himself and calmly put the ball in the net. Just a couple of minutes later Hamilton repeated his burst, got away from the defenders and this time finished it himself to make it 2-0 to Rangers. Despite Killie's terrific effort, the game had swung Rangers way and could not be retrieved.

It had been a valiant attempt by Killie to lift the cup, but it was not to be. Perhaps, on reflection, Rangers just had that little bit of extra class in certain positions when it was required. Killie's normally devastating left wing of Reid and Findlay had not really performed to their full potential, although Reid had in fact injured an ankle and would miss the remaining League matches.

Division Two champions Kilmarnock had shown what they could do, but it was still not enough to gain the club election to Division One for the following season. However, so dominant were they in the following season (1898/99) that they ran away with the Division Two championship again, going undefeated in all League games, and for the second season in a row winning all home League fixtures. Division One could surely not be denied them again. It wasn't.

Scottish Cup finalists 1897/98. From left to right, back row: J.Q. McPherson (Trainer), D. McPherson, T. Busby, J. McAllan, R. Brown, J. Johnstone. Front row: R. Muir, D. Maitland, J. Campbell, G. Anderson, W. Reid, R. Findlay.

Kilmarnock: McAllan, Busby, Brown, McPherson, Anderson, Johnstone, Muir, Maitland, Campbell, Reid, Findlay.
Rangers: Dickie, N. Smith, Drummond, Gibson, Neill, Mitchell, Miller, McPherson, Hamilton, Hyslop, A. Smith.

St Mirren v. Kilmarnock

Date: 19 August 1899 **Match title:** Scottish League Division One
Location: Love Street, Paisley

After securing the Division Two championship in 1898/99 Kilmarnock FC was belatedly elected to Division One (there was not yet automatic promotion and relegation in operation). For their first-ever Division One game they did not have too far to travel. A special train took around 700 Killie fans to Paisley to cross swords with St Mirren, who had been members of the top flight since the League's inception in 1890. St Mirren had knocked Kilmarnock out of the Scottish Cup at the quarter-final stage 2-1 the previous season and this had been hugely upsetting to everyone at Rugby Park. Killie were definitely on a revenge mission.

Rain had threatened in the morning, but by afternoon it was warm and sunny. In the absence of Jocky Johnstone, Tom Busby was elevated to the captaincy and he won the toss. Saints kicked off towards the end furthest from the pavilion in front of around 5,000 spectators. Early on the teams seemed well matched, as play went from end to end. Killie's Howie (later to play for Newcastle United and Scotland) missed a great chance when he knocked the ball over the bar when scoring seemed easier. As the first half wore on, Kilmarnock began to take control. Their forwards seemed much sharper than those of the home team and the famous 'Bummer' Campbell grazed the top of the bar, but then, in a Saints breakaway, Busby was deemed to have shouldered his opponent off the ball and a penalty kick was awarded to the home team. Steel struck the kick hard and straight, but 'keeper Alex Craig, who had advanced from his line as was allowed at that time, made a magnificent save at the expense of a corner. This save was greeted by wild cheering from the Kilmarnock fans – to them, Craig was a hero. From the resultant corner Killie broke upfield and Reid found himself in a scoring position. Bruce attempted to trip him, but he kept his balance and knocked the ball into the net. However, the referee had blown for a Killie free-kick, much to Reid's disgust. Minutes later Killie again netted, but again it was disallowed. This time Campbell was ruled to have 'infringed' against goalkeeper Patrick. Hard to believe – surely the legendary 'Bummer', a shrinking violet if ever there were one, would never have done such a thing! 'Bummer's' next involvement saw him carry the ball forward and release a pass to Findlay who ran in on goal and shot. The ball finished up inside the net, but how had it got there? Referee Neilson never hesitated and immediately awarded a goal, but Patrick claimed that the ball had come through the side of the net. Other St Mirren players then took up the call and the match was held up for fully five minutes as they protested against the award of a goal. The referee stood his ground and would not be moved, even after examining the nets. He may also have been influenced by the fact that, as one report described it, 'the ball was lying in front of goal where one of the home backs in disgust kicked it into the back of the net'. We will never know now exactly how it was, but the goal stood. From the kick-off Killie attacked yet again, and Howie tried to walk the ball round the 'keeper, but Patrick literally lifted it off his toes. Thus the score remained at 1-0 to Kilmarnock at half-time. The home side now had the breeze at their backs and tried desperately to force an equaliser. Saints' Young, making his debut, had the ball in the net but he had clearly been offside. Killie now seemed content to hold on to their one-goal

---

St Mirren 0   Kilmarnock 1
                                     Findlay

Left: George Anderson. A rock-solid centre half for Killie and Scotland. Had two spells at the club between 1897 and 1909. *Middle:* Robert Muir. Bobby was a right-winger who played for Killie between 1897 and 1901. Won a Scottish Cup medal with Celtic in 1904. Moved to Canada and was later heavily involved in arranging Kilmarnock's 1930 tour of Canada and the USA. *Right:* Robert Findlay. Pencil-slim Rab was a brilliant left-winger capped once by Scotland. Played for Killie from 1897 to 1900 when he transferred to Celtic. Injuries hampered his career badly.

advantage and they did, with Anderson in particular being most impressive, especially in the air. Killie generally looked the more likely team all through and the final whistle saw them happy to have started off life in Division One with a deserved away win. However it was not quite all over. St Mirren captain Michael McAvoy, born and bred in Kilmarnock, had intimated to the referee at the time of the goal that he wished to register a protest, and after the game Mr Fairley of St Mirren handed the referee the swiftly written protest. This was duly considered, but was inevitably rejected and the result stood. Kilmarnock had their first 2 points in Division One football. At the end of this season the club finished in fifth position in the League, while St Mirren finished eighth.

One final thought – surely the home side is responsible for the fitting and condition of the goal nets? It is not known if checking the nets was part of a referee's duties at this time, but I would suspect that it was. In any event, St Mirren, as the host club, could be said to have been negligent in this matter, although if the ball did pass through the outside of the net, they still had grounds for grievance. We will never know, but the referee thought it was a goal and to quote an old saying, often used when a team disputes the result: 'If you want to argue about the score, just check the Sunday papers!'

St Mirren: Patrick, Neil, Jackson, Hastings, Bruce, McAvoy, Chalmers, Steel, Young, Orr, Wyllie.

Kilmarnock: Craig, Busby, Brown, McPherson, Anderson, McCrone, Muir, Howie, Campbell, Reid, Findlay.

KILMARNOCK v. CELTIC

Date: 26 August 1899   **Match title:** Scottish League Division One
Location: Rugby Park

On this day, what was without doubt one of the most significant football occasions in the history of Kilmarnock Football Club took place. Quite possibly it was the most significant of all! Never before or since can one Killie game have had so many important aspects attached to it. Even the timing of the match seemed to have a certain symbolism – people were already looking towards a new century dawning and were hopeful of a better world in the coming twentieth century (although as we now know this was not necessarily to be, as it was to bring two cataclysmic world wars). Kilmarnock Football Club was certainly looking towards a bright new future, as this was the club's first season of Division One football and the first-ever home match at that level. The Division Two Championship flag, won by Kilmarnock in the previous season, was also to be unfurled and, by a great stroke of good fortune or perhaps smart work by the fixture planners, the visitors for this occasion were no less than the famous Glasgow Celtic, the holders of the Scottish Cup, Glasgow Cup and winners of the Glasgow League (the latter two competitions were still considered significant competitions at that time). All this, though, was outweighed by the inauguration of the new, extended Rugby Park that was to have its grand opening on this day. Kilmarnock had played for many years on the wide expanse of Rugby Park, with the actual playing pitch moving its location several times over those years. Now, however, 'Greater Rugby Park' had been established. The pitch was re-sited (to the position where it remains to this day) and lengthened, the enclosed area was enlarged by five acres and a running track was created around the pitch. The pitch itself was extended and another stand capable of holding 1,500 people had been erected. Regrettably, a joiners' strike meant that some of the work had not been completed in time for this game, but it was sufficiently advanced not to cause any serious difficulties. The ground was intended to host athletics and sports meetings as well – indeed a 'Highland Games and Sports Meeting' was scheduled to take place the following Saturday. The grand opening included marching bands and a large parade watched by the local dignitaries and merchants as well as footballing VIPs such as Mr McAndrew, secretary of the Scottish League and the vice-president of the SFA Mr Kirkwood, who hoisted Killie's Championship flag. Then they all crowded round with the two teams to take their place in the official photograph to commemorate this momentous day. A special train had run from St Enoch Station in Glasgow; it was the week of the Trades Holiday in the city and close upon 1,500 journeyed to the 'Land of Burns'. An estimated crowd of over 11,000, huge by the standards of the day, witnessed the kick-off shortly after the advertised time of four o'clock. Every precaution had been taken by the Kilmarnock executive to prevent confusion or disorder, and it was gratifying that everything worked out so successfully. The first kick-off, to inaugurate the new pitch, was taken by Mr Gairdner of the Union Bank, which was supplying much of the finance for the ground developments, and then the ball was brought back to the centre where, appropriately, Killie legend James 'Bummer' Campbell then set the game in motion for real. Kilmarnock

Kilmarnock 2	Celtic 2
Howie (2)	*Divers*
	Marshall

The twenty-two players rub shoulders with officials, dignitaries and VIPs prior to the big match on 26 August 1899.

unfortunately had to take the field without their inspirational half-back, the vastly experienced David McPherson, a Scotland international who had been taken ill during the previous week. Thomas McCrone, who had stood in for Jocky Johnstone a week before, now found himself standing in for McPherson this time.

The initial impression given when the two teams took the field was that the Celtic side was much heavier than their Kilmarnock counterparts, but it was Killie who were first on the attack, winning a corner. From the corner a great shot from Reid hit the inside of the post, with some of the Kilmarnock players claiming, unsuccessfully, that the ball had actually gone over the line. Three more corners for the home team followed in the next three minutes, but Celtic survived this opening bombardment. Celtic then got into gear, and when Killie's Busby miskicked, an error that was blamed on the blinding sun he was facing, Jack Bell had a chance, but Brown got across to knock the ball out of play. Then Harry 'Beef' Marshall had Celtic's first real shot at goal, and it only just cleared the crossbar. Celtic were enjoying a good spell and it culminated in the opening goal with less than twenty minutes played. Clever work by Sandy McMahon and John Divers created a chance, and the latter shot past Craig. Some thought that Craig might have saved the shot, but the sun was again felt to have had something to

Kilmarnock: Craig, Busby, Brown, McCrone, Anderson, Johnstone, Muir, Howie, Campbell, W. Reid, Findlay.

Celtic: McArthur, Welford, Turnbull, Battles, Marshall, King, Hodge, Campbell, Divers, McMahon, Bell.

do with his failure to do so. Shortly afterwards Bell smacked a fine shot against the Killie crossbar, and the Celts pushed forward only to find themselves being thwarted on several occasions by Johnny Hodge's tendency to run into offside positions. However, a second goal for Celtic was not long in coming. Killie captain Johnstone was penalised for a foul against Divers a few feet outside the penalty area, and from Marshall's kick the ball found the net. It should be noted at this point that in 1899 the laws decreed that a goal could not be scored directly from a free-kick, but the referee, Mr Hendry from Linthouse, judged that the ball had grazed the top of Johnstone's head and awarded the goal, much to the disgust of the home supporters. Even though two goals down, Kilmarnock were not daunted and Campbell led the way as they forced Celtic back into defence, but luck was not with them, evidenced by an incident near the interval when a Busby free-kick found its way into the Celtic net, but this time no second touch was spotted by the referee and the teams retired to the dressing rooms with the score 2-0 in favour of the visitors.

In the early stages of the second half it was Celtic who dominated, and they missed a few chances, but, on one of the hottest days of the year, it was the much heavier Celtic players who began to show signs of distress and appeared to be wilting in the heat. The home side, looking much fitter, took control of the match and exerted heavy pressure.

The Kilmarnock half-backs, particularly George Anderson, who was superb, pushed forward as some of the Celtic heavyweights came almost to a standstill. Around the sixty-minute mark Reid, Findlay and Campbell combined brilliantly to force a corner that outside-left Rabbie Findlay, who later joined Celtic, swung in, McArthur pushed out, Johnstone sent back in, and Campbell controlled the ball before sending it to James Howie, and from a difficult angle Howie squeezed it into the net. The cheers must have been heard miles away. A minute later Findlay grazed the crossbar as Campbell lay in the back of the net. The Killie pressure intensified – Anderson and Divers, who had been having a running battle all through the match, clashed again and a free-kick was awarded to

James 'Bummer' Campbell was a legendary figure with Killie from 1888 to 1901. His goals tally for the club can only be roughly estimated as scoring records are incomplete for the earlier years. It could be as high as 200, but the fearless 'Bummer' was much more than just a goalscorer. He could play almost any position and was capped by Scotland in 1891 and 1892.

William Reid. 'Roggie' Reid was a skilful forward who had a reputation as a bit of a rascal. He had a spell at Newcastle in 1899. His brother Andrew also played for Killie.

Kilmarnock. Anderson lobbed the ball into the goal area and it was headed out, but only as far as Jocky Johnstone who returned it to Howie, who scored with a shot which gave goalkeeper Daniel McArthur absolutely no chance of saving his superb overhead kick. The scenes that followed beggared description, although one report did suggest, somewhat improbably, that 'even the horses of the mounted police danced for joy'. The visitors' defence was now sorely pressed to hold out. Howie got through to hit the bar. Then Campbell drove in a shot that McArthur stopped but could not hold, and the in-rushing Findlay lashed it into the net. To the amazement of the crowd the referee disallowed the goal, presumably for offside, but the unanimous verdict after the game was that this was not possible. It was thought that what was possible was that Howie might have been offside earlier in the move, but as the referee had allowed play to proceed at that point, he could hardly give offside now that the ball was in the net. Nevertheless the final whistle sounded with the result a 2-2 draw, reflecting enormous credit on newly promoted Kilmarnock, who had been very unfortunate not to take both points. McArthur in goal had been the Celts' star man. King, McMahon and Divers had also played well, but it was the Rugby Park men who took most of the plaudits on this momentous day, as the team had got their First Division career off to an excellent beginning in their brand-new ground.

QUEENS PARK v. KILMARNOCK

Date: 15 December 1900　　　　　　**Match title:** Scottish League Division One
Location: Hampden Park

Kilmarnock visited Hampden Park for the first time on League business on a wild and windy December day. This was Queens Park's first season in the Scottish League having stuck to their principles for a decade during which they had refused to take part with the 'professionals'. Although they had now joined the League they were still holding fast to their amateur status, as indeed they have done right up to the present day, even though Queens are fully aware of just how much of a disadvantage this gives them. They were still a force to be reckoned with in 1900; indeed they had reached the Scottish Cup final in the previous season, losing only 4-3 to Celtic.

Killie went into this game on the back of a terrible result the previous week at Tynecastle. A 7-0 defeat produced four changes in personnel; Busby, McPherson, Wyllie and Howie all came in to replace Mitchell, Anderson, Morton and William Reid. In addition, Bobby Muir, who had played at right-back against Hearts, reverted to his more usual position of outside right.

Killie won the toss and decided to take wind advantage in the first half. How very significant this was to prove to be! The visitors forced three corners in quick succession, but they proved fruitless. However, Kilmarnock's sustained pressure produced a goal in twenty minutes. A fine Hugh Woodburn pass put Davie Maitland in, and he swiftly netted. A second goal soon followed – this one was credited to Andrew Reid, the younger brother of William 'Roggie' Reid, one of the players dropped for this match. Play continued to surge around 'keeper McWattie and a third goal came as no surprise, so one-sided was the play. This time Johnny Graham dribbled right through the home defence and scored. A sprint downfield from Queens' left-winger McLean momentarily relieved the siege, but with a chance to score, he shot wide. Play was soon back at the other end and goal number four came when Reid passed to Graham, who netted his second goal. With half-time approaching, a scramble took place right in front of the home goal, McWattie failed to hold on to the ball and it was forced over the line. The credit for this fifth goal was given to Graham, thus completing his hat-trick and giving an astonishing half-time score of Queens Park 0 Kilmarnock 5.

The home side came out for the second half hopeful of being able to at least restore a degree of respectability to the scoreline now that they had the benefit of the prevailing wind. It was Alex Craig's turn to come under pressure and in the early stages he showed himself to be well up to the task. However, what had been a strong wind in the first half had now become something approaching a hurricane. Ten minutes into the second half Queens' legendary international striker, R.S. McColl (the founder of the confectionery business of the same name) pulled one goal back, deflecting in Wilson's shot. Within a minute Clarkson had added a second and the home fans began to get excited. Despite the wind, Killie broke away and Muir hit a good shot, but McWattie managed, with some difficulty, to save and then did likewise from a Howie effort. Inevitably a third goal for Queens was not long delayed and this one was credited to Wilson. Straight from the kick-off the dangerous McColl was in again and made it 5-4, creating great excitement,

---

Queens Park 5
McColl (3)
Clarkson
Wilson

Kilmarnock 5
Maitland
Reid
Graham (3)

particularly in the covered stand. The fifth and equalising goal came with fully twenty minutes still left. It was awarded to McColl, although other sources gave it to McGhee. Whoever got the last touch, the Queens Park fans did not care as they went wild. Some of the Killie players claimed that the ball had not actually gone through the goal, but had gone through the side of the net, but just as had happened in the St Mirren v. Kilmarnock game in the previous season, the referee, Mr Phillips of Glasgow, allowed the goal. By a quirk of fate, now that the teams were level with fifteen minutes to go, the hurricane-force wind that had blown during the second half died down to something like the strength it had been throughout the first half. Despite the home fans' promptings, it was Kilmarnock who took the initiative in the later stages and were denied a penalty kick when Graham, about to shoot for goal, was pushed over. Killie finished the match strongly and almost succeeded in regaining their lead against all the odds. Perhaps a draw was the right result though for this remarkable League encounter.

Despite this game taking place on 15 December, Killie had only three more League matches to play afterwards; their final League encounter of the season took place on 1 January 1901. The second half of the season was taken up with Scottish Cup and West of Scotland League matches. Kilmarnock repeated their League position of their first season, fifth, while Queens Park finished eighth in the eleven-team Division One.

David Maitland was with Killie from 1897 to 1902. As an eighteen-year-old he played against Rangers in the 1898 Scottish Cup final.

Queens Park: McWattie, Swann, Russell, Irons, Clarkson, Templeton, D. Wilson, McGhee, McColl, Kennedy, McLean.
Kilmarnock: Craig, Busby, Agnew, McPherson, Wyllie, Woodburn, Muir, Maitland, Graham, Howie, A. Reid.

Port Glasgow Athletic v. Kilmarnock

Date: 4 January 1908   **Match title:** Scottish League Division One
Location: Clunie Park, Port Glasgow

This match may not truly qualify for the description of 'classic', but it certainly qualifies as one of the most unusual League matches ever. Kilmarnock played with only seven players. I don't mean that they lost four men through injury or sendings off – Killie actually started and finished this game with just seven players. The circumstances conspiring to cause this occurrence are long and involved.

Saturday 4 January 1908 was, as is not particularly unusual at that time of the year in Scotland, a bitterly cold, frost-bound day. Curling and skating were taking place on New Farm Loch. Kilmarnock FC faced a trip to Port Glasgow for a League encounter, but the expectation was that the game was unlikely to take place and postponement was almost certain. The local Port Glasgow Athletic were bottom of the League with a meagre total of 9 points from 22 matches, Killie were in twelfth place in the eighteen-team League with 16 points. The severe weather (the temperature was 20°F), frost and a thick fog conspired to cause the cancellation of most trains, and those that did run were subject to very lengthy delays. The delays meant that four Killie players missed their connection at Glasgow Central Station for Port Glasgow. The players wired ahead to the Kilmarnock FC secretary to inform him that there was no possibility of them reaching Clunie Park by kick-off time; however, they would take the first available train. The players asked to have the Greenock train make an unscheduled stop at Port Glasgow, but this was refused and it became clear to them that they would be lucky if they made their destination before the end of the game, never mind the start. At this point they probably made a wrong decision. In the belief that in all likelihood the game would be called off anyway, they took themselves off to a pantomime in Glasgow! Meanwhile a pantomime of a rather different kind was taking place at Clunie Park.

By agreement, the kick-off was delayed by twenty-five minutes to allow the errant players time to arrive, but when they still had not shown up a start was made. Killie lined up with half-back William Shaw in goal and James Mitchell, David Walker, George Anderson, David Howie, Alex Wilson and Robert Barton doing their best to fill all the outfield positions. The four missing men were goalkeeper Stuart Strachan, full-back William Agnew, half-back George Halley and winger Bobby Templeton. Their absence was a severe loss; Agnew and Templeton both appeared for Scotland that season, and Halley later won an FA Cup-winner's medal with Burnley in 1914 and clearly the absence of Strachan meant the team had no specialist goalkeeper. In fairness to Port Glasgow they were extremely considerate towards Killie's plight, particularly as they were involved in a relegation battle (which they ultimately lost). Apart from allowing the kick-off to be delayed, they offered assistance to Kilmarnock in the way of loaning players, but owing to League registration rules Killie felt unable to accept the offer. So Killie started with only the seven, but still naively believing that the missing players were on their way and that they would soon be at full strength. Not altogether surprisingly, Edgar opened the scoring for 'Port' in the first minute, but amazingly seven-man Killie cashed in on some casual play by their opponents to equalise through Howie. The home side's Ritchie missed a penalty kick but then MacDonald scored to put 'Port' back in front

---

Port Glasgow Athletic 4
Edgar, MacDonald
Hill, Ruddiman

Kilmarnock 1
Howie

From left to right: two who played against Port Glasgow, David Howie and James Mitchell, and two who should have but didn't, George Halley and Bobby Templeton. By the time of the picture cards, Howie and Halley had moved to England.

and they led 2-1 at half-time. This could be viewed as a pretty decent score for Kilmarnock in the circumstances, but in all truth the home fans were unhappy, and felt that they had been cheated of a spectacle. Many were seen to leave at half-time. Kilmarnock made a change and put Barton in goal and Shaw switched to play outfield. Early in the second half Athletic scored twice through Hill and Ruddiman, and from then until the end of the game they contented themselves with playing exhibition football. Before the finish the ground had almost emptied. The one sure thing was that Kilmarnock Football Club had some explaining to do, as a furore blew up in the press. The club's directors held a meeting on the Tuesday night to enquire into the reason for the non-arrival of the players and Killie's secretary, W. Barrie Grieve, was obliged to write an extremely apologetic explanatory letter to the Scottish League. In the end the match result stood and the whole affair was quietly allowed to drop. I doubt though if the League was told where the missing players had actually spent their Saturday afternoon!

Port Glasgow Athletic: Thomson, Steel, Ritchie, Cunningham, Ross, Bulloch, Hamilton, MacDonald, Ruddiman, Hill, Edgar.
Kilmarnock: Shaw, Mitchell, Walker, Anderson, Howie, Wilson, Barton.

CELTIC v. KILMARNOCK

Date: 21 April 1917   **Match title:** Scottish League Division One
Location: Celtic Park, Glasgow

It has never been easy for Kilmarnock to win at Celtic Park. At Rugby Park Killie's record is not too bad, but throughout the years wins at Parkhead have been few and far between. April 1917 most certainly was not a good time to be visiting Glasgow – Celtic had not lost a League match since November 1915, a run of 62 matches without defeat, the British record for an unbeaten run in senior league football to this day. They had been Scottish Champions for four consecutive seasons, including the one just ending, and even though Killie themselves had enjoyed a reasonable season, finishing sixth in a twenty-team League, hopes were not high of success in this, Kilmarnock's last League game of the 1916/17 season.

Killie were considered unfortunate not to have ended Celtic's unbeaten run two months earlier at Rugby Park on 24 February. On that occasion it took an equaliser a couple of minutes from time to make the score 2-2 when Tom Sinclair, an ex-Rangers and Celtic 'keeper, making his debut for Killie on loan from Newcastle United, fumbled a McMenemy shot. The teams took the field at Celtic Park before a crowd of approximately 18,000 fans at a time when the First World War was dominating the thoughts of most people. Newspapers were filled with long lists of 'Death Notices' from the Western Front and stories of food shortages on the home front. Football must have provided one of the few outlets from the mood of prevailing sadness that gripped Britain. The Scottish League, unlike the English version, continued to function throughout the war, but it was in a much scaled-down form, with one division only, while the Scottish Cup had been abandoned until hostilities ceased.

In the opening stages of the game Celtic not unexpectedly took the initiative, forcing several corners, which Killie goalkeeper Tom Blair dealt with in a most confident manner, coming out of goal to catch or punch away the ball. It was clear that Tom was on his very best form and this conveyed itself to the rest of a youthful Kilmarnock team. After about twenty minutes, during which Celtic had largely dominated, but looked weak when it came to finishing off their pretty moves, the tide began to turn. To be fair, Celtic had been unlucky not to score – Dodds and McStay had both gone close with free-kicks and Blair had performed brilliantly. The Killie half-back line of Henderson, Goldie and Mackie was the driving force behind the turnaround in play. Celtic by comparison appeared inferior at half-back, and for the remaining twenty-five minutes of the first half the visitors took over. Celtic's McMenemy, dubbed 'the Master', had been prominent in those early stages but he completely faded out of the game. The breakthrough for Killie came when a long ball was played through, it seemed that Celtic 'keeper Charlie Shaw was coming out to collect it, but he hesitated and Mattha Smith was able to chip the ball past him. More Killie pressure followed and a fine shot by left-winger Malcolm McPhail, older brother of Rangers player Bob McPhail, produced an excellent save from Shaw, which partially redeemed the 'keeper for his error at the goal. A second goal was not long delayed however. Seven minutes before the interval Killie broke down the right wing. Fulton only just managed to catch the ball before it went out of play, but he cut in and squared the ball across goal. Celtic's McNair and Shaw plus

Celtic 0   **Kilmarnock 2**
                                            Smith
                                            Culley

Killie's Culley were in the middle, and as the ball came over it appeared as if McNair was trying to touch it back to his 'keeper, but he found himself colliding with a goalpost and impeding Shaw at the same time. Willie Culley was left with the simple task of knocking the loose ball over the line and found himself credited with the second goal (although some reports suggested that the ball was already over the line before he touched it). In any event it was a most curious mix-up, leaving Kilmarnock ahead 2-0. Early in the second half it should have been three when McPhail was left with simple tap-in, but elected to blast it and missed the target altogether. Celtic attempted to come back again and created a few more opportunities in the later stages, but Blair was always up to the task of thwarting them and a fine young Kilmarnock side took the points. Celtic's long unbeaten League run had ended, but their players took the defeat in a most sporting manner. Thus fell to Kilmarnock FC the honour of ending the longest unbeaten run in League football. The following season Killie improved further and finished third in the League, while Celtic had to make do with second spot in 1917/18 after their four championships in a row. The men credited with the Killie goals were highly appropriate in that Willie Culley and Mattha Smith are the highest and third-highest Kilmarnock League goalscorers of all time, and they would both go on to win cup-winner's medals with the club in the near future.

Left: Tom Blair, whose brilliant goalkeeping inspired the team at Parkhead. *Right:* John Goldie, who also starred in the 2-0 victory over Celtic.

Celtic: Shaw, McNair, Dodds, Wilson, McStay, Brown, McAtee, Gallagher, McColl, McMenemy, Browning.
Kilmarnock: Blair, Mitchell, Patrick, Henderson, J. Goldie, Mackie, Fulton, Smith, Culley, Rutherford, McPhail.

KILMARNOCK v. ALBION ROVERS

Date: 17 April 1920
Location: Hampden Park

Match title: Scottish Cup Final

With the First World War now over, but clearly not forgotten, life began to return to something like normal and this included the return of Scottish Cup football. A tournament had been held along the lines of the cup in 1918/19, but it was not the real thing, being termed the 'Victory Cup', and was seen as merely a temporary substitute until things were back to normal. St Mirren had beaten Hearts in the Victory Cup final of 1919, but unfortunately for the Saints, this excellent triumph is considered unofficial and is not listed among the Scottish Cup winners. Therefore 1920 represented the first Scottish Cup final since 1914, and the finalists were Kilmarnock and Albion Rovers. The 'Wee Rovers' were the shock team of the tournament, having disposed of the League Champions of this season, Rangers, in the semi-final. Although they had a poor season in the League, Rovers held the mighty Ibrox men to 0-0 and 1-1 draws before prevailing 2-0 at the third attempt. So nobody was writing them off when it came to a final against Killie, who were themselves competing in their first Scottish Cup final since the 1898 match against Rangers. Albion Rovers had proved themselves great battlers, especially in those three games against Rangers.

Despite that, Killie fans were confident that they would bring the cup back to Ayrshire for the first time. The perception was that Kilmarnock had a greater degree of skill in their line-up, and that this would outweigh the pluck that the Albion Rovers team undoubtedly possessed. A large number of special trains left Kilmarnock for Glasgow on the day of the game, with many more supporters following on by road, using whatever means of transport could be found. It seemed to be the case that only women and small children were left to look after the town for the day! Or as one wag put it, only the statue of Sir James Shaw and a dog to watch it was left. So great was the interest in this final that the authorities seemed to be caught out and could barely handle the number that turned up. The gates were finally shut when an estimated 95,000 people were inside. This was a greater number than Hampden could accommodate properly

Two of Killie's cup-final heroes: Mattha Shortt (*left*) and Tom Hamilton (*right*).

Kilmarnock 3
Culley
Shortt
J.R. Smith

Albion Rovers 2
Watson
Hillhouse

Another two of Killie's cup-final heroes: Willie Culley (*left*) and John Reid Smith (*right*). These two, along with Mattha Shortt, shared the Killie goals.

at that time, and consequently many of the spectators inside saw very little of the actual play. It was a new record attendance for a club match in Scotland; only the Scotland v. England international match of 1912 was believed to have had a larger crowd up until then. (The highest attendance for a final before this was the estimated 70,000 who saw the 1909 'Old Firm' game.) Including tax, £4,521 (£3,391 after tax) was taken at the gate and it was from this that the actual attendance figure in 1920 was calculated, although quite how the number who forced their way in without paying was estimated is not known. Computerised turnstiles were still a long way in the future!

The weather was all that could be desired; glorious sunshine met the teams when they came out onto the field. Rovers had two enforced changes from their victorious semi-final side; Wilson and Black replacing Noble and Duncan at right half and centre half respectively. Kilmarnock fielded the same eleven as they had when they disposed of Morton in their semi-final. It was underdogs Albion Rovers who attacked early on and they were extremely determined and aggressive, as expected, and with only five minutes on the clock they took the lead when Wilson pushed the ball to James White, who evaded Neave and then passed out to Ribchester. Ribchester crossed perfectly and Watson was there to find the net with a fine shot, giving Blair no chance. The scorer Gavin 'Guy' Watson was actually an ex-Killie player, he played for the club from 1912 to 1913, but had been born in Coatbridge and was thus representing his home-town team in this game. Killie tried to hit back immediately, and after some good play Mattha Smith crossed the ball into the Rovers goalmouth and J.R. Smith got his head to it but sent it just over the bar. This was soon followed by a vociferous Killie penalty-kick claim for handball, but it was turned down and the Rovers survived. Kilmarnock would not be denied however, and with just fifteen minutes gone they got an equaliser when Willie Culley beat both Penman and Black and clipped a beauty into the net. The Rugby Parkers now took a firm grip on the match and dominated until half-time, particularly in the final ten minutes of the half when they swarmed around the Rovers goal, but they could not add

---

Kilmarnock: Blair, Hamilton, Gibson, Bagan, Shortt, Neave, McNaught, M. Smith, J.R. Smith, Culley, McPhail.

Albion Rovers: Short, Penman, Bell, Wilson, Black, Ford, Ribchester, James White, John White, Watson, Hillhouse.

KILMARNOCK v. ALBION ROVERS

The 1920 Scottish Cup Final squad. From left to right, back row: J. McAdam, H. Wilson, H. Spence (secretary), R. Russell, R.H. Thomson. Third row: W.C. Cunningham, P. Carrick, T. Hamilton, T. Blair, D. Gibson, J. McWhinnie, A. Gibson. Second row: J.L. Morison, J. McNaught, M. Smith, J.R. Smith, W. Culley, M. McPhail, C. Smith. Front row: A. Mackie, M. Shortt, R. Neave, J. Bagan.

to their tally, sturdy full-backs Penman and Bell proving real obstacles. During the first half, Rovers, to their credit, had played flat out, but the suspicion was that Kilmarnock seemed to have a little something extra left in reserve.

Three minutes into the second half this theory appeared to be confirmed when Killie took the lead. Shortt set his forwards going yet again, as indeed he did throughout the match, Mattha was not a centre half in the way we would understand it today, he belonged to the school of attacking centre halves who played just slightly behind their forwards, for such was the norm in those days, before the later introduction of the 'stopper' centre half. Mattha knocked the ball forward and kept going himself, and then latched on to the return pass from J.R. Smith and made no mistake as he crashed it past his namesake in the Rovers goal. The referee turned down the Coatbridge team's appeals for offside. Within just eight minutes we had another goal as the brave Rovers fought back to equalise. Wilson slung a ball across the field towards Hillhouse, Killie full-back Tom Hamilton should have intercepted but seemed to think that the ball would go out of play, left it, and was horrified when Hillhouse appeared on the scene and hit a beautiful slanting left-foot shot past Blair. The score now stood at 2-2 and Rovers' tails were really up, as for the next ten minutes they enjoyed what was probably their best spell of the whole game. They might have scored again on several occasions, but Tom Blair was in excellent form, indeed he was transferred to Manchester City for a large fee a month later, but he was perhaps just a little fortunate on one occasion when his outstretched left foot turned away a John White shot which was heading for the net. Kilmarnock came through this awkward spell unscathed and got back on top, and at the midway point in the second half, following good build-up play by Bagan and Culley, the outstanding J.R. Smith dribbled through brilliantly and struck a superb left-foot shot home for what was considered by many people to be the goal of the match. J.R. Smith later won two FA Cup-winner's medals with Bolton in 1923 and 1926, scoring in the first of those games against West Ham United in the first-ever FA Cup final played at Wembley.

Rovers, naturally, never gave up and tried their hardest to equalise again but it was now beyond them. They did come close a couple of times, but it was clear that Killie just had that bit more class, as the two clubs respective League positions at the end of the season confirmed, Killie finished eighth and Albion Rovers finished twenty-second of the twenty-two clubs then in the top division, and they deserved their hard-won victory even though the brave men from Coatbridge had pushed them all the way. The outstanding Killie inside forward trio of Mattha Smith, John Reid Smith and Willie Culley was probably the strongest part of the team and the key to their victory, but Blair, Shortt and Gibson were other star performers. For Hugh Spence it was a marvellous triumph in his first year in charge of Kilmarnock Football Club. One unfortunate moment marred an otherwise wonderful day when Killie's Shortt and referee Bell from Hamilton were involved in an undignified altercation, which did neither of them any credit.

Provost Smith had arranged a 'civic welcome' for the returning heroes at Kilmarnock Town Hall, despite the fact that 'out-of-town' business prevented him from being there in person. The Burgh Band and Burgh Fire Brigade turned out dressed in the club's colours. At the railway station a three-horse charabanc was waiting for the team, and when they arrived in Kilmarnock at 8.35 p.m. they were met with wild outbursts of cheering from thousands of people. The players were carried shoulder-high to their carriage, but it was an extremely difficult passage to the Town Hall as all routes were jam-packed and progress was very slow, but who really cared? Once there, Baillie Jones, standing in for the Provost, tried to make a speech, but could not be heard above the din. Everywhere was blue and white. The first final after the First World War had seen the blue riband of Scottish Football come to Kilmarnock for the first, but not the last, time.

KILMARNOCK v. CELTIC

Date: 23 March 1929   **Match title:** Scottish Cup Semi-Final
Location: Ibrox Park

Despite injury worries, Kilmarnock went into this game very confident. However, until a few days before the match, the composition of the team was doubtful. Rugged centre half 'Jake' Dunlop, badly injured on 12 March against Partick Thistle, was out for the rest of the season, and top scorer Harry 'Peerie' Cunningham and scheming inside forward Jimmy Ramsay were also ruled out. Centre half was the main problem position, as suitable deputies were available for the two forwards, namely James Weir and Jimmy Williamson, but not for Dunlop. After trying several clubs without success, Killie managed to secure a loan of Aberdeen's reserve centre half Hugh McLaren (something not possible under today's rules). McLaren was actually an Ayrshire man born in Kilbirnie. Celtic had not enjoyed a particularly successful season in the League – although finishing second, the forwards had not found consistent form, and this was shown by the fact that of the top eleven teams at the end of the season, only ninth-placed St Johnstone scored less League goals than Celtic's 67.

Matthew Smith, known as 'Mattha', the only survivor from Kilmarnock's 1920 Scottish Cup-winning team, led out his side before an estimated crowd of 40,000. He won the toss and elected to take the benefit of the prevailing breeze, something which appears to have been considered much more important in those days than today. Killie's McEwan had their first attempt on goal, but his shot went wide. Soon after, from Paterson's corner, Williamson back-heeled the ball and Celtic's defence just managed to scrape it clear. The Rugby Parkers were well on top at this stage, with Celtic defending desperately to keep them out. Smith was a very conspicuous figure, but he was guilty of a bad miss, failing to get the final touch on Paterson's cross when all that was required was to push it over the line. The main threat to Killie came from speedy right-winger Paddy Connolly, a particular favourite of the Celtic fans at this time. Connolly broke away and his fast low cross almost found Jimmy McGrory, but Robertson got there first to clear the danger. Celtic's biggest fright so far came when Hugh Morton dispossessed Scarff, carried it forward and his shot dropped in front of 'keeper John Thomson. It kicked up viciously and the astonished goalie only just managed to turn the rising ball over the bar. With twenty-four minutes gone Killie made the breakthrough. Connell accepted Smith's pass, beat full-back McGonagle and crossed to where Weir was ideally positioned to tuck it into the net. Killie then survived a scare when McLaren sent the ball back to his 'keeper a little too strongly, but Clemie coped. Paterson, always a source of danger, was heavily fouled at the edge of the box when about to shoot, but referee Craigmyle rejected penalty-kick claims. McGrory then got away from McLaren for the first time, Clemie came out and as McGrory shot for the corner of the net, Sam threw himself and tipped it away brilliantly. At the other end Paterson beat Willie McStay and crossed towards Connell, who looked sure to score until Thomson dived low and smothered the ball. The score remained 1-0 at the break

Celtic now had the benefit of the breeze and attacked aggressively, determined to make up for their poor first-half show. However, Killie's defenders performed so well that Clemie had little reason for anxiety. Then Smith sent Connell away and

---

Kilmarnock 1   **Celtic 0**
Weir

the little fellow centred nicely; Paterson did his best to clinch matters, but could not get enough on the ball. Paterson was proving a handful for Wilson and McStay, and when he next beat McStay he was fouled by the defender as he went past yet still managed to send the ball into the net, but the whistle had sounded to award the free-kick. Next McGrory took a typically powerful header, worthy of a goal, and brilliantly saved by Clemie. Then came probably the closest thing to a goal since Weir's strike. Thomson came out for Paterson's cross but Connell got his head to it first and the ball scraped past the post with the goal empty. With the finish drawing near, Celtic made renewed efforts to equalise and the Killie fans had a couple of scares, especially when Robertson's goal kick went straight to Connolly, and Clemie was forced to run out of goal to kick it away. Kilmarnock survived and the final whistle saw them worthy 1-0 winners.

It was a typically hard-fought, but nevertheless clean cup tie. Celtic never dominated at any time, even with the wind, as Killie had done in the first half. Killie's half-backs were outstanding, much better than Celtic's on the day, and McGrory crucially did not play to his best form. John Thomson, who was brilliant, had been much busier than his counterpart Clemie, who had only three moments of anxiety during the whole game. Any doubts about stand-in defender McLaren proved groundless, and he received congratulatory telegrams from his Aberdeen colleagues. Paterson had possibly the best game of his Kilmarnock career. McEwan had the hardest task in matching the speedy Connolly, but Jock was superb. To their credit the Celtic players gave hearty handshakes to their opponents at the end, taking their defeat in true sporting fashion as Kilmarnock went through to their third final.

Matthew 'Mattha' Smith, who served Killie from 1916 to 1931, was captain of the 1929 team. Mattha was born in Stevenston, Ayrshire, in 1897 and died in Glasgow in 1953 and was one of Kilmarnock's greatest ever players. His 415 League appearances puts him fifth in the club's all-time list, while his 109 League goals makes him Killie's third-highest League scorer of all time.

Kilmarnock: Clemie, Robertson, Nibloe, Morton, McLaren, McEwan, Connell, Smith, Weir, Williamson, Paterson.

Celtic: J. Thomson, W. McStay, McGonagle, Wilson, J. McStay, Donoghue, Connolly, A. Thomson, McGrory, Scarff, Gray.

Kilmarnock v. Rangers

Date: 6 April 1929   **Match title:** Scottish Cup Final
Location: Hampden Park

Having disposed of one half of the much-celebrated 'Old Firm' in the semi-final, it now fell to Kilmarnock to attempt to dispose of the other half in the Scottish Cup final. Rangers, the League Champions for the third consecutive season (and they would win it again in the next two as well) had beaten St Mirren 3-2 in the other semi-final at Hampden, and needless to say Rangers were hot favourites to retain the trophy, which they had won a year before by beating Celtic 4-0 in the Hampden final. On their way to the final stage Kilmarnock had disposed of Glasgow University 8-1 at home, Bo'ness 3-2 at home, Albion Rovers, old final rivals from 1920, 1-0 away, Raith Rovers 3-2 away and Celtic 1-0 in the semi-final at Ibrox. Killie had played against Celtic in their semi-final without the services of Dunlop, Cunningham and Ramsay, and now Danny Paterson, who had played a starring role in the semi-final, was out with illness. John Aitken was brought back into the team to replace Paterson at outside left and top scorer Harry 'Peerie' Cunningham came back in place of the injured James Weir at centre forward. The same players who had defeated Celtic filled the other nine places.

114,708 fans passed through the turnstiles on the day of the 1929 Scottish Cup final, with many more locked out. Only the previous year's 'Old Firm' final had produced a larger crowd until then. It was a fine sunny day, spoiled only slightly by a strong breeze. Rangers won the toss and, as seems to have been standard practice in those days, took advantage of the wind (and the sun, in their opponents' faces) in the first half.

The first Rangers attack saw Sandy Archibald cross the ball, and it bounced dangerously in front of goal, but Clemie managed to punch it clear. In Kilmarnock's first attack Williamson passed to Aitken, who raced down the left wing, but his subsequent cross was not good enough to cause any danger. Then a free-kick for Rangers twenty-five yards out did cause problems. A mêlée in the goalmouth ended only when Sam Clemie dived in and grabbed the ball to loud cheers from the Killie fans. Rangers were now getting on top and were making sweeping raids, one of which led to Clemie holding on to a powerful McPhail shot. Kilmarnock were making only occasional raids into Rangers' territory. With fifteen minutes gone Rangers were awarded a penalty kick. Jock Buchanan pushed forward, beating several opponents, and just as he was about to shoot, Killie's Hugh Morton tackled him and he fell. Opinion was divided as to whether or not it had been a fair tackle, but referee Tom Dougray pointed to the spot. The Killie players protested and Mr Dougray decided to seek a second opinion. He went over and spoke to a linesman and came back and prepared to restart play with a drop-ball. The Rangers players then protested, so he went to the other linesman and came back and awarded a penalty kick again! Craig took the kick, but this was Sam Clemie's day, and putting all the refereeing nonsense behind him, he threw himself to bring off an astonishing save from Craig's full-blooded drive to thunderous cheers. Killie took heart from this; they had been under severe pressure, but now they attacked much more. From Connell's corner Smith had a good try on target that was blocked. However it was still Rangers who had most of the play and Clemie had to make another good save

---

Kilmarnock 2   **Rangers 0**
Aitken
Williamson

Outside Hampden. From left to right: Alex Smith, an ex-Rangers player born in Darvel, Ayrshire; Charles Smith, former Chairman and player with Kilmarnock; Hugh Spence, then Kilmarnock secretary-manager and John Greenaway, former Kilmarnock chairman.

from a Muirhead header, and then McEwan blocked a netbound Archibald shot with his body. Just before the interval McPhail, whose older brother Malcolm had played for Kilmarnock in the 1920 final, had a great opportunity when the penalty-kick hero Clemie made a rare slip, palming the ball out to him. The crowd held its breath as McPhail steadied himself and then gasped with astonishment as he knocked it over the bar. Rangers never had as good a chance again throughout the rest of the match. Kilmarnock were happy to go in at the interval all square, having had to absorb so much Rangers pressure.

Killie now had the sun and wind at their backs, and it took them only four minutes to do what Rangers had failed to do in the whole of the first forty-five minutes, and score! Hugh Morton drove the ball hard into the Rangers goal area from the right wing, giving Rangers goalkeeper Tom Hamilton only enough time to stick out a foot to deflect the ball away. It went directly to the incoming John Aitken who whacked it straight back into the net, to his great joy. Rangers and their fans

Kilmarnock: Clemie, Robertson, Nibloe, Morton, McLaren, McEwan, Connell, M. Smith, Cunningham, Williamson, Aitken.
Rangers: T. Hamilton, Gray, R. Hamilton, Buchanan, Meiklejohn, Craig, Archibald, Muirhead, Fleming, McPhail, Morton.

were stunned by this reversal and although the Ibrox side had a chance when Fleming lifted the ball just a foot over the bar a few minutes after Killie's goal, Rangers never looked like the same powerful combination as before the goal, and it was a now confident Kilmarnock who did most of the attacking. Twice they had the goal at their mercy, first when Willie Connell set up Cunningham, but 'Peerie', who had scored 34 League goals in the previous season (still the Kilmarnock League record for one season, only equalled by Andy Kerr in 1960/61), knocked it past the post and then Williamson, who had exhibited superb touches throughout, sent a long pass out to Connell for him to run in and crack the ball off the crossbar, only for Aitken to strike the rebound wide. Rangers full-back Gray then pulled down Williamson inside the box, but no penalty kick was given. With around a quarter of an hour left for play came the clincher. The masterful Williamson, who was signed only two years before from Ardrossan Winton Rovers but played like a veteran, controlled a Connell corner kick and slung a wicked left-foot shot through a crowd of players and into the net. The Killie players and fans were ecstatic, Rangers were demoralised, and it could have been 3-0 when Williamson again sent in a fine shot which Hamilton just managed to save. The match finished on a sour note when Rangers' robust right half Jock Buchanan became the first player ever to be sent off in a Scottish Cup final following an 'unfortunate altercation' two minutes from full-time. It was suggested that Buchanan had used 'unbecoming' language to the referee.

Surely this was the ultimate way to win the Scottish Cup, beating Celtic in the semi-final and Rangers in the final! Thousands of delighted people, just as in 1920, met the team on its return to the town that evening. The Burgh Fire Brigade, who

Referee Tom Dougray looks on as the two captains, Mattha Smith of Kilmarnock and Tommy Muirhead of Rangers, shake hands before the 1929 cup final. Mattha's grandson, Gordon Smith, later played for both clubs and scored for Brighton in the 1983 FA Cup final.

Left: Sam Clemie clears; in the background are Tommy Robertson (Kilmarnock) and Bob McPhail (Rangers).
Right: Jimmy Williamson, who always looked too skinny to be a footballer. He scored the second goal in the 1929 final.

had one of their engines brightly decorated, and the Burgh Military Band escorted them all along the route to the Grand Hall, where a reception had been arranged for them. The crowds cheered the players vociferously and Provost Jones offered his sincere congratulations on their glorious triumph, and intimated that the town council was making arrangements to entertain them in a suitable manner. A reception and dinner took place soon after in Lauders Restaurant, hosted by the council. In addition the rotary club had entertained the players and officials at dinner on the Thursday following the final. Messrs Henderson the Jewellers supplied monogrammed watches to all eleven players plus the chairman, Andrew S. McCulloch, the secretary/manager Hugh Spence and the trainer John McWhinnie. Happily, permission was also received for the four injured players, 'Jake' Dunlop, James Weir, Jimmy Ramsay and Danny Paterson, who had all missed the final, to be awarded cup-winner's badges along with the secretary/manager and the trainer.

KILMARNOCK v. RANGERS

Date: 18 February 1933   **Match title:** Scottish Cup Third Round
Location: Rugby Park

Kilmarnock Football Club maintained its excellent record in the Scottish Cup following the final triumphs of 1920 and 1929 by reaching the semi-final in 1931 (losing to Celtic) and the final again in 1932, when they once more faced Rangers. However, this time Rangers gained revenge for 1929, although it was only after a 1-1 draw, with Killie considered unlucky not to have triumphed, that the Ibrox side prevailed. The clubs were drawn to meet each other yet again the next season, 1932/33, but this time it was in the third round and took place at Rugby Park. Great excitement was generated in Kilmarnock by the draw, and the talk was of a new record-attendance figure for the ground being set. Despite Kilmarnock being recognised as formidable Scottish Cup opponents, Rangers were nevertheless still favourites to qualify for the next round. On the day, the crowd figure did indeed constitute a new record for Rugby Park. The previous best had been 31,502 for another Scottish Cup tie against Rangers, on 7 March 1925. The new record was 32,745, although some reports gave the figure as 32,505.

The Kilmarnock side showed no less than six changes from that which had faced Rangers in the final a year before, with Milliken, Milloy, Glass, Liddell, Sneddon and Gilmour replacing Bell, Nibloe, Morton, Connell, Muir and Duncan respectively. Rangers showed four changes from the side that had won the replay; Dawson, McDonald, Main and Smith had taken the places of T. Hamilton, McAulay, Archibald and McPhail. The visitors opened strongly and twice Fleming got centres across, but Killie's Tom Smith saw them safely out of danger. 'Bud' Maxwell then fastened onto Milloy's clearance and sped away before passing to Liddell in a promising position until McDonald got across to clear. A minute later Marshall had the best chance so far – a pass from Sam English allowed him to run in on goal, but his powerful shot was blocked by Milliken's outstretched leg. At this point English was showing exasperation with Killie's offside trap and Rangers were beginning to falter after a strong opening spell. Killie's Leslie and Glass seemed to have got over their early nerves. Then Simpson headed the ball against his own crossbar and Dawson was forced to scramble it away with Sneddon close at hand. Tom Smith was the dominant figure at the heart of the Kilmarnock defence as he repeatedly broke-up Rangers attacks, spoiling fine play by Main and Marshall. Two chances fell to Aitken; the first he put wildly past the post but the second was on target and saved by Dawson. Killie were beginning to get the upper hand and when, with thirty-seven minutes gone, Jock McEwan sent another long ball up the middle, bisecting Simpson and McDonald, young Liddell on Killie's right wing got onto it, dashed in towards goal and hit a powerful shot into the net, giving Jerry Dawson no chance. Liddell was smothered by his delighted comrades. At the interval the score stood at 1-0.

From the kick-off at the start of the second half, Killie showed that they had no intention of sitting tight on their one-goal lead. Gilmour ran through and passed to Sneddon, but he missed an easy chance to make it two. Rangers hit back when a free-kick was awarded against Gilmour, and Meiklejohn placed the ball into the middle where Smith got his head to it but Milliken managed to save. John Aitken,

---

Kilmarnock 1   **Rangers 0**
Liddell

on Killie's left wing, broke away at great speed and got clear in on goal, but shot straight at Dawson and a good chance was gone. Kilmarnock were now well on top and were showing great confidence. Marshall was now the only Rangers man offering a threat, but he could not get past the Killie rearguard on his own. 'Bud' Maxwell was injured when he challenged Simpson and Dawson, and he had to go off the field for a few minutes, however, when Bud returned he soon had two chances but missed both. Next it was Gilmour's turn to miss a chance to clinch matters when he ran into the box and shot just wide with Dawson helpless. The home fans were now wondering if Kilmarnock would live to regret all these missed opportunities. However, they need not have worried as they had a fairly comfortable time; Rangers just could not seem to raise themselves to find an equaliser and Killie ran out convincing winners, even if it was only 1-0.

It was a great day for Kilmarnock after a shaky first fifteen minutes. Milliken had relatively little to do, while Jimmy Leslie was magnificent at full-back. Tom Smith was probably the best man on the field, Jock McEwan inspired his colleagues and young Liddell never shirked an encounter with McDonald or Brown, as well as netting the only goal. Maxwell kept Simpson guessing throughout and while Gilmour had a poor first half, he fully atoned in the second. Dawson, Gray and Marshall were Rangers' best men. Apart from those first fifteen minutes of the game and the first ten minutes of the second half, Rangers' forwards offered little threat to the Kilmarnock defence. Killie had their revenge for the 1932 cup final.

Left: William Liddell, scorer of the only goal of the game. *Right:* Tom Smith, an inspiring figure at centre half for Killie in 1933. He later captained Preston to victory in the 1938 FA Cup final.

Kilmarnock: Milliken, Leslie, Milloy, Glass, T. Smith, McEwan, Liddell, Sneddon, Maxwell, Gilmour, Aitken.
Rangers: Dawson, Gray, McDonald, Meiklejohn, Simpson, Brown, Archibald, Marshall, English, Smith, Fleming.

KILMARNOCK v. AIRDRIE

Date: 23 September 1933   **Match title:** Scottish League Division One
Location: Rugby Park

On a fine September day Kilmarnock faced Airdrie in their tenth League match of the season. Killie's exciting young centre forward James 'Bud' Maxwell, the idol of the fans, had just been picked to represent his country for the first time at senior level. He was in the team to play against the Irish League in Belfast and no wonder – in the nine League games played by the club so far he had scored in the first eight, and had missed out only on the ninth when Killie drew 1-1 in an away match against Third Lanark the previous Saturday. Bud, Kilmarnock born and bred, was the son of a former Killie, Sheffield Wednesday and Woolwich Arsenal player of the same name, who lost his life in the First World War when Bud was only three. The club had kept an eye on him from an early age, and he was taken on the tour of North America in the summer of 1930 as a seventeen-year-old, and played his first games for the first team there. His League debut came on 6 September 1930 at Motherwell when he came in for Harry 'Peerie' Cunningham, who was nearing the end of his Killie career. Soon he was hitting the net on a regular basis – his first League strike came two weeks later at Paisley – and from then on he continued scoring at a rate which kept his many fans happy, including the goal in the 1-1 draw against Rangers in the 1932 cup final. By the time of this Airdrie match, Maxwell was twenty years old and had played exactly 100 League games for the club (scoring 79 goals) and 18 Scottish Cup ties (17 goals). Much was expected of him and he was about to deliver.

Willie Connell, who had played in the 1929 and 1932 cup finals, was back in the team for his first League match since a serious injury against Aberdeen on 5 November 1932. The home side which faced a strong sun, started off in businesslike fashion. Maxwell passed to Connell, but his cross was cleared, then, with just seven minutes gone, it was the visitors who scored in their first serious attack. Duffy eluded McEwan and Milloy and sent the ball across to the unmarked Mooney (also in the team for the game against the Irish League) and his first-time shot went over the line, despite 'keeper James Miller appearing to save but then letting it slip under his body, injuring a finger in the process. Kilmarnock immediately set about chasing an equaliser; Morrison held a Keane shot and then pushed a long one from Milloy away for a corner. However, with still only ten minutes gone, Kilmarnock scored when Williamson sent the ball across to John Keane who smashed it home. Two minutes later referee T. Small awarded Killie a free-kick for a foul on Maxwell. Jock McEwan shot powerfully and the ball flew past Morrison, taking a slight deflection off one of his defenders. The visitors employed offside tactics to counter Maxwell, and this displeased the home fans, but Airdrie to their credit tried to hit back, and for a spell it was end-to-end, with Airdrie's wingers looking dangerous and creating chances of their own, but the score remained 2-1 for Killie until half-time.

On the resumption Mooney was causing problems on the left wing, but the cool Tom Smith was able to clear up any danger created, and then his mate Maxwell decided it was time he took a hand in proceedings. Jimmy Williamson found Connell, who crossed to Maxwell. Bud almost lost the ball but quickly recovered, warded off both full-backs and the 'keeper and slipped it into the net. Minutes later,

---

Kilmarnock 7
   Keane (2), McEwan
   Maxwell (3), Connell

Airdrie 1
   Mooney

This 1933/34 team group contains nine of the eleven players who took part in the 7-1 win over Airdrie. This picture was actually taken at Firhill on 19 August 1933. From left to right, back row: J. Glass, T. Smith, H. Morton, J. Miller, F. Milloy, J. McEwan. Front row: W. Liddell, J. Williamson, J. Maxwell, W. Kennedy, J. Keane.

McEwan's adroit lob from the left found Maxwell, who resisted a challenge and struck home an unsaveable rising shot from almost thirty yards. Two more minutes and he completed his hat-trick with the best goal of the trio. Glass put Bud through to run in unchallenged and he made absolutely no mistake. Maxwell had scored three goals inside five minutes! Indescribable scenes followed as the stand rose en masse and acclaimed him.

Airdrie were now well beaten and Bud came within a whisker of scoring again from Connell's cross. Six minutes from time John Keane hit a powerful right-foot shot which took a deflection off Sharp on its way past the helpless Morrison, and with one minute left Connell took the score up to 7-1 following a McEwan free-kick. Kilmarnock had dominated the second half, apart from when Mooney, Airdrie's best player on the day, hit a post with a great shot. Killie's best performers were the tireless Andrew Kelvin, silky Jimmy Williamson plus McEwan, Keane and Connell. However, above them all this day was the sensational Bud Maxwell, with his hat-trick inside five minutes. Unfortunately only 5,352 fans saw it.

Kilmarnock: Miller, Morton, Milloy, Glass, Smith, McEwan, Connell, Williamson, Maxwell, Kelvin, Keane.
Airdrie: Morrison, Calder, Shaw, Thomson, Sharp, Todd, Duffy, Grant, Moore, Harrison, Mooney.

KILMARNOCK v. AYR UNITED

Date: 2 January 1936
Location: Rugby Park

Match title: Scottish League Division One

On Thursday 2 January 1936 a struggling Ayr United team visited Rugby Park on League business. United were engaged in a battle against relegation to Division Two and were, even more than is usual in a derby match, desperate for the points. They had lost their two previous matches 6-1 against Rangers at Ibrox and then 3-1 at home to Queen of the South. They were to be sadly disappointed, for their rearranged team was to be completely outclassed and seriously outplayed again.

The opening exchanges did not suggest the debacle that was to come, but once Kilmarnock settled down there was never any doubt as to the ultimate destination of the 2 points. After fifteen minutes Killie's Welsh left-winger Sam Roberts crossed for Jimmy Robertson to head past Bob Hepburn, although it was suggested that the ball might have gone out of play before Roberts crossed it, but Ayr's claims for a goal kick were rejected. Just four minutes later Robertson scored again from a pass slipped through by the astute Jimmy Williamson. This time Ayr's claims for offside met with the same response as those for the first goal, as the referee again saw nothing wrong. Ayr's nearest approach to a goal came when Jimmy Leslie almost headed into his own net, but his fellow full-back Andy Fyfe cleared the ball off the line. With thirty-one minutes gone Killie went three goals in front. Roberts ran into position to take a cute Bobby Beattie pass, and drove the ball in from an acute angle, giving Hepburn no chance. Ayr had never really looked like scoring themselves in the first half, and they appeared to be particularly weak in the half-back positions as they went in at the interval 3-0 down and very dispirited.

Ayr's ex-Rangers forward James Fleming and Terry McGibbon, signed from Irvine Meadow, swapped positions for the second half and this seemed to bring about an immediate improvement as, one minute after the resumption, Fleming, now playing at centre forward, scored a really well-taken goal, although goalkeeper James Miller got his hands to it but let it slip past him. Five minutes later, when Fyfe failed to trap the ball and let it skid under his foot, Fleming was again alert enough to drive the ball high into the net. The score was now 3-2 and the home players and fans were stunned that after such domination they were now only one goal ahead. At this point the highly talented and enigmatic Bobby Beattie, who had been relatively subdued until then, decided that he had better take a hand in the proceedings. Beattie and his wing partner Roberts virtually took over the game. Killie extended the lead again by making the score 4-2 when Sammy Ross's driven free-kick was diverted by Williamson's head and flew into the net. It had been a quite deliberate action by the intelligent Killie player and showed what a quick thinker he could be to react so instantly. Beattie then ran from the halfway line, beating four opponents, but instead of netting the goal of the match he knocked it past the post when heavily challenged. The bold Bobby was not to be denied for long and on seventy minutes he scored goal number five after Hepburn had only partially saved from Jimmy Robertson. Sam Roberts, signed from Rangers the previous October, had possibly his best ever game for Kilmarnock and it was he who, with two excellent crosses, set up Robertson for two more goals on seventy-three and eighty-two minutes. Ayr simply could not cope with the little genius Beattie when he decided to start

---

Kilmarnock 7
Robertson (4), Roberts
Williamson, Beattie

Ayr United 2
Fleming (2)

Seven of this eleven took part in the 7-2 victory over Ayr United. From left to right, back row: T. Smith, M. Kenmuir, J. Leslie, W. Brown, F. Milloy, S. Ross. Front row: B. Thomson, J. Williamson, J. Robertson, R. Beattie, J. Keane.

playing. In the end it finished 7-2 and could well have been a great deal more. Hepburn had actually played well in goal for Ayr, but the rest of the team had struggled badly and Fleming, with his two strikes, was the only other Ayr man who could be awarded pass marks. Clearly it was not a happy new year for Kilmarnock's 'first-footers'. United's struggles continued right through to the end of the season, but they failed to escape the dreaded relegation, finishing bottom of the twenty-team division, but at least they were spared the ignominy of losing a century of League goals. They restricted the tally to 98 against them. Kilmarnock finished the season in eighth place in the League.

Kilmarnock: Miller, Leslie, Fyfe, Milliken, T. Smith, Ross, Thomson, Williamson, Robertson, Beattie, Roberts.
Ayr United: Hepburn, Bourhill, Strain, Currie, Watson, Holland, Fleming, Dimmer, McGibbon, Steele, Tough.

CELTIC v. KILMARNOCK

Date: 5 March 1938   **Match title:** Scottish Cup Third Round
Location: Celtic Park, Glasgow

The first half of season 1937/38 must rank as one of the poorest ever endured by Killie's faithful fans. Many of the outstanding players of the early thirties, such as Mattha Smith, Joe Nibloe, Hugh Morton, Jock McEwan, Willie Connell, Tom Smith and James 'Bud' Maxwell had departed, and replacements of the same quality were proving difficult to unearth. By late November, manager Hugh Spence was asked to resign, which he eventually did very reluctantly, and in December legendary Celtic goalscorer Jimmy McGrory, who had just announced his retirement as a player, was appointed Kilmarnock manager. When he took charge, the club had played 20 League matches, winning only 4 and drawing 5. They had scored 31 goals and conceded a crippling 52, and no 'clean-sheets' had been kept.

The twenty-first League match (Jimmy McGrory's first in charge) was played at Parkhead against his former club on Christmas Day of 1937. It came as no surprise that Killie lost this match, but the margin of the defeat, 8-0, must have given the new manager quite a shock. However, a few judicious changes and some reorganisation of the available resources over the next few weeks brought about an amazing turnaround. From New Year's Day 1938, Kilmarnock lost only 1 of the next 10 League and cup matches, taking the team into a third round Scottish Cup tie at Celtic Park on 5 March 1938. The whole scenario read like a Hollywood film script: Jimmy McGrory, the all-time Scottish League record goalscorer with 410 League goals, was to take his new club to visit his old club, who were top of the League and had already beaten his new club 8-0 in his first match. Despite Killie's improved form since that thrashing, nobody outside of Rugby Park gave them a chance of beating the table-toppers. Celtic, on a run of 19 games without defeat, had not lost at home for over a year.

The much-fancied Celtic side kicked-off amid a buzz of excitement. It was their Jubilee year, fifty years since their founding in 1888, and the club was determined to do the League and cup double to celebrate this landmark. Celtic played this match in green jerseys with white sleeves and collars, rather more representative of modern-day Hibernian, but they were to find that their opponents on this day represented a far more formidable threat than the Kilmarnock side they had played on Christmas Day.

Killie started very promisingly and outside right Benny Thomson had the first shot of the match, which was cleared. George Reid, a tall inside forward, who was actually on loan from Celtic to Kilmarnock (presumably Jimmy McGrory must have seen something in him when he was at Parkhead) was very prominent in the early stages. The match opened at a furious pace, and players from both sides went into tackles with 'sleeves rolled up', but although it was tough it was an extremely clean affair. Johnny Hunter's first save was from a powerful shot by Malky MacDonald which he held down at the base of the post. MacDonald incidentally later played for, and then became manager of, Kilmarnock some years later. Jimmy Delaney, Celtic's Scottish international right-winger, had a good opportunity but his drive as the ball came over from the left was skied high over the bar. Killie's next attack was to bring great joy to their huge travelling support: a throw-in by George Robertson

---

Celtic 1
MacDonald (pen)

Kilmarnock 2
McGrogan
Collins

48

Malky MacDonald, who scored Celtic's goal from a penalty kick. Malky later played for Kilmarnock and was their manager from 1950-57 and again from 1965-68.

to Thomson started the move after thirteen minutes, and it ended when a cross from the right wing was met by the incoming outside left Felix McGrogan, who headed it past Joe Kennaway into the net off the inside of the post. Celtic now realised just how much they had underestimated their opponents. Killie received a huge boost from the goal, and Ross and Robertson were now winning the ball in midfield and continually feeding it through to their forwards. In defence, young centre half Jackie Stewart was containing the lively Johnny Crum, and he refused to be drawn out of position. At this point scoring chances for the home side were few and far between. A second goal for the visitors should have come shortly after the first, but nineteen-year-old Dougie McAvoy held the ball too long when a pass to Allan Collins would have put twenty-year-old Collins through on goal. Tenacious tackling by Stewart and full-backs Andy Fyfe and Freddie Milloy meant that young goalkeeper Johnny Hunter, although a little nervy in some clearances, was seldom called upon as Killie kept control of the match.

Ten minutes before half time a Killie free-kick reached Thomson via Reid and his cross from the right was miskicked by Celtic full-back John Morrison. Collins was onto it like a shot, and as Kennaway rushed out to close him down Allan coolly knocked the ball past him. Pandemonium broke out among the Killie fans; Sammy Ross was to comment after the game that 'when Collins scored our second goal I thought the stand was falling on us'. Two up and Kilmarnock kept going forward, almost getting another goal when a header by McGrogan found Collins again, and he was pulled down well inside the box, but referee J.M. Martin of Ladybank refused Killie's appeals for a penalty kick to be given. Play again surged around Kennaway, and a smashing shot by McGrogan bounced off Bobby Hogg for a corner, and then another escape followed as Reid headed against the bar. This was the last incident in a thrilling first half that saw Killie go in at the interval with a sensational 2-0 lead.

Celtic restarted in determined fashion, and applied sustained pressure for almost the first time in the game, but the Kilmarnock defence withstood it heroically. Crum had a

---

Celtic: Kennaway, Hogg, Morrison, Lynch, Lyon, Paterson, Delaney, MacDonald, Crum, Divers, Murphy.
Kilmarnock: Hunter, Fyfe, Milloy, Robertson, Stewart, Ross, Thomson, Reid, Collins, McAvoy, McGrogan.

good chance, but again he sent it past the post. Quick tackling by Fyfe and Milloy, who did not stand on ceremony, was particularly effective. Milloy was injured, but it didn't affect his defensive work, as he stuck doggedly to his task against the speedy Delaney. The Celtic forwards were playing well, but just could not penetrate the visitors' defence. However, on fifty-seven minutes came the break the home side were after when Fyfe, in attempting to clear his lines, inadvertently hit the ball with his arm, and a penalty kick was awarded. Malky MacDonald gave Hunter no chance from the kick and the deficit was now reduced to one. As the Celts pushed forward desperately for the equaliser, Killie found opportunities to counter-attack presented to them on several occasions. Wide passing movements engineered by Reid opened up the Celtic defence, and one of these breaks ended with McGrogan hitting a rocket shot which cannoned off Kennaway's shoulder and flew over the bar for a corner. A similar occurrence took place at the other end; a great shot by Frank Murphy struck Hunter's knee and it too went for a fruitless corner.

The Celtic support was now getting worked up, with hugely vociferous backing as their side pushed for the all-important equaliser, but it would not come. Back

Allan Collins, scorer of the second goal against Celtic.

Cup-training smiles at Rugby Park. From left to right: F. Milloy, A. Collins, B. Thomson, G. Robertson, J. McWhinnie (Trainer), D. McAvoy, S. Ross.

on the offensive, Killie won a corner, and as Benny Thomson was taking it the referee stood with his watch in his hand and, when the corner was cleared and Killie prepared to take the resultant throw-in, the final whistle sounded. Kilmarnock had won a glorious victory by two goals to one. At the end the blue-and-white-capped Killie fans burst through the police cordon and mobbed the Killie players with their congratulations, and it was with some difficulty that Sammy Ross and his gallant men reached the shelter of the pavilion. It had not been a case of snatching a goal and hanging on – they had shown no inferiority complex. Kilmarnock, with only four full-time players in their ranks and an average age of only twenty-two, had defeated the favourites, the holders of the trophy and the team who would take the League Championship at the end of the season, scoring 114 League goals along the way. 39,389 fans had been thoroughly entertained by a sparkling match full of honest endeavour and hair's-breadth escapes at both ends, yet clean throughout, even though full-blooded tackling was a feature of the game.

In Andy Fyfe, Kilmarnock had the outstanding defender on the field, and his commitment compensated for the fact that his full-back partner Freddie Milloy had been injured early on and had limped through the majority of the game. The other defenders, particularly young Stewart at centre half, had done their bit to withstand the second-half pressure. Reid in midfield had supplied great service to Thomson and Collins throughout, and ensured that as much as possible of the play took place in Celtic's half of the field. Celtic were denied the League and cup double; they did win the League Championship in their Jubilee year but it was Kilmarnock who went forward to the fourth round of the Scottish Cup, where they were delighted to find they had been drawn to play at home against the winners of the Morton v. Ayr United tie.

Ayr United v. Kilmarnock

Date: 23 March 1938   **Match title:** Scottish Cup Quarter-Final Replay
Location: Somerset Park, Ayr

Kilmarnock had defeated Celtic in the Scottish Cup third round, and county neighbours Ayr United had overcome Morton 4-1 after a 1-1 draw to set up an Ayrshire derby fourth round (quarter-final) to be played at Rugby Park on 19 March 1938. A Benny Thomson goal just before the half-hour mark gave Killie the lead, but six minutes into the second half Ayr's Taylor equalised from a free-kick. A remarkable crowd of 28,595 had turned up for this game despite the threatening nature of the weather. The game had finished 1-1 and a replay was scheduled for Somerset Park on Wednesday 23 March 1938.

So great was the interest in the replay that another excellent attendance of 23,785 turned up at Somerset Park on the following Wednesday afternoon. Kilmarnock fielded the same eleven as in the first match while Ayr manager Frank Thompson announced only one change, with Newall replacing Thow on the left wing. Now that they had the home advantage, most pundits were of the opinion that United were now favourites. In the early stages it seemed that these pundits might be correct as the home side swept forward towards John Hunter, and the first attack ended with Steele shooting over the bar. In Ayr's next attack they won a free-kick, and then forced a corner. It was clear that they were all out for an early goal. Then the wonderfully-named Hyam Dimmer created an opening for himself, but delayed shooting and his chance was gone. All this inside the first ten minutes, but Kilmarnock began to settle and took up the attack, and it was Ayr's turn to defend as Hall was forced into a brilliant save from Thomson. Then, with still only eleven minutes gone, McAvoy was fouled by Ayr's Taylor. Sammy Ross knocked the free-kick into the box, and there was McAvoy to meet it and send a header past Hall. United tried to hit back and Terry McGibbon beat Milloy and hit a rocket-shot at Hunter, who managed to divert it away for a corner with his leg. It was now end-to-end stuff as the sides strove for supremacy. Then came a controversial moment, with the home side awarded a penalty kick when, with Yardley and Milloy on the ground tangling for the ball, Milloy was deemed by the referee to be holding it between his legs. It seemed a harsh ruling, but in the event it mattered little, as Hunter brought off a fine save from Currie's penalty kick. Ayr appeared to lose heart from this miss and Killie gained confidence from this point onward. McAvoy had a great run, beating

Dougie McAvoy. Kilmarnock born, he headed the first goal at Ayr. He played a few games for Liverpool after the Second World War.

Ayr United 0	Kilmarnock 5
	McAvoy, Collins
	Thomson (2, both pens)
	McGrogan

Goalkeeper Johnny Hunter, who kept a clean sheet at Somerset Park.

several men and shooting, only for Hall to produce a fine save. Towards the interval Killie had the best of matters, but when the whistle blew for half-time it remained only 1-0 to the visitors. Ayr were not too upset with this score, as they felt that with the wind at their backs in the second half they still had an excellent chance of pulling off a victory. One cloud on their horizon was the number of free-kicks Ayr had been conceding; indeed the only goal so far had come as a result of a free-kick.

The early part of the second half saw Killie having to absorb some Ayr pressure, but they survived and took play to the other end, and six minutes after the interval the visitors won yet another free-kick. Milloy placed it on Allan Collins' head, and Allan placed it in the corner of the Ayr net. Just one minute later the game was all but over. Dyer fouled Collins in the area and from the spot Benny Thomson made it 3-0 to the joy of the huge Kilmarnock support. Ayr did not give up, but Killie now had a firm grip on proceedings and when another penalty kick, the third of the game, was awarded in the sixty-second minute, when Dyer this time pulled down Reid, it was a formality for Thomson to make it 4-0. Five minutes from the end it was no surprise when McGrogan took a cute pass from McAvoy and smashed a low shot past Hall. It was 5-0, and in the end Ayr had not been in the same class as Kilmarnock. The Ayr defence, particularly Davie Currie, had proved stubborn, but up front Killie had been shown to be far superior. Only McGibbon of the Ayr forwards had offered any real threat. It was Kilmarnock who would go forward to meet Rangers in the semi-final (up to this time Ayr United had still never made the semi-final, indeed they did not do so at all until 1973). Killie would go to Hampden in a fairly confident mood having beaten Rangers in a League match as recently as 12 March at Rugby Park. They had now gone 10 matches without defeat, 8 wins and 2 draws. It was a great time to be a Kilmarnock supporter!

Ayr United: Hall, Dyer, Strain, Taylor, Currie, Mayes, McGibbon, Dimmer, Yardley, Steele, Newall.
Kilmarnock: Hunter, Fyfe, Milloy, Robertson, Stewart, Ross, Thomson, Reid, Collins, McAvoy, McGrogan.

Rangers v. Kilmarnock

Date: 2 April 1938   **Match title:** Scottish Cup Semi-Final
Location: Hampden Park

Kilmarnock went into this semi-final having extended their unbeaten run to 11 matches, including Scottish Cup victories over Celtic and Ayr United as well as a 2-1 League victory over semi-final opponents Rangers. Despite being again written off as having 'no chance' by the city press, with their ultra-enthusiastic team of youngsters Killie's confidence was high.

The weather was unkind, raining very heavily all morning, and until half an hour before kick-off it was still pouring down, and only in the later stages of the game did the sun appear. The ground was left very heavy, muddy and sticky and this was perceived as being an advantage to the more powerful Rangers team. The foul weather was also responsible for keeping the crowd down to only 70,833 when many more had been expected.

Rangers began well and Brown's through-pass forced Hunter to come running out to clear from Willie Thornton, and shortly after a long-range shot from McPhail flew just wide. Then, from a Sammy Ross throw-in, Collins ran in on goal, but rushed his shot and it also went past the post. There was still only six minutes played when Rangers took the lead. Main made the opening and young Thornton netted from close range, the ball going in off the post. Rangers were now playing well and seemed certain winners, as they appeared to have a grip of the Kilmarnock forwards. Hunter was repeatedly called upon to deal with shots, and fortunately for Killie he dealt with them in a very confident manner. Gradually Kilmarnock worked their way into the game, with Allan Collins' harassing of Rangers' centre half Jimmy Simpson (father of Celtic's Lisbon Lion, Ronnie Simpson) particularly noteworthy, given that Collins must have been about 5ins shorter than Simpson. Up until now Killie winger Benny Thomson had seen little of the ball, but when he did he made good use of it, beating Alec Winning cleverly, cutting in and from a tight angle driving for goal, but 'keeper Jerry Dawson flung himself across goal to turn it away for a corner. Sammy Ross was also becoming prominent in the Killie midfield, providing great service to those in front, and the tide slowly turned. On twenty-five minutes Killie equalised. McAvoy, seen little until now, slipped the ball to McGrogan, and Felix skipped past Gray and sent in a cross. It seemed to be Dawson's all the way, but Collins nipped in front of him to head the ball down and followed it into the net. It was a brilliantly taken goal, leaving Jerry Dawson the most surprised man at Hampden.

Naturally this setback triggered an immediate response from Rangers. McPhail ran through the defence, but Johnny Hunter again saved his shot. Even though Rangers were doing the bulk of the attacking, the Killie forwards were always dangerous. Rangers, with the wind at their backs, had not taken their chances and Kilmarnock, thanks mainly to Hunter, happily went in level 1-1 at half-time.

Killie restarted promisingly. George Reid had a good opportunity but delayed his shot, giving Gray time to clear. Centre half Jackie Stewart was the man who mattered most in keeping Rangers away from Hunter, and managed to keep the dangerous Thornton relatively quiet. Main's cross then hit the post and was cleared away. Eleven minutes into the second half McGrogan got the ball, and just as with Killie's

---

Rangers 3
Thornton
Venters (2)

Kilmarnock 4
Collins (2)
Thomson (2, 1 pen)

Allan Collins heads Killie's first goal in the semi-final against Rangers.

first goal, he rounded Gray and crossed into a packed goalmouth. The ball was scrambled away, but only as far as Benny Thomson, who was standing clear waiting for just such a break, and he thumped it into the Rangers net. This was a staggering blow to Rangers, but the Killie fans were in 'seventh heaven'. Their joy was short-lived however, as from the restart Rangers ran straight through the Killie defence and Alex Venters beat Hunter with a powerful shot, without a single Kilmarnock player touching the ball. Inside sixty seconds the score had gone from 1-1 to 2-2. The match continued at an amazing pace. Collins and McGrogan ripped Rangers' defence open, but George Brown stepped into the breach to save the day. Then Milloy

---

Rangers: Dawson, Gray, Winning, McKillop, Simpson, Brown, Main, Venters, Thornton, McPhail, Kinnear.
Kilmarnock: Hunter, Fyfe, Milloy, Robertson, Stewart, Ross, Thomson, Reid, Collins, McAvoy, McGrogan.

Programme for the 1938 cup final against East Fife.

prevented Thornton getting a shot in as the pressure once again mounted on Killie, but with seventy minutes gone Rangers once more took the lead. Bob McPhail intercepted a pass and placed it beautifully for Venters to rush in and shoot past the helpless Hunter. The Killie players were undaunted and swept down on their opponents goal, forcing three corners in quick succession. Then, with around thirteen minutes left, real drama! Simpson of Rangers and Killie's Collins had many duels in this game and when they tangled once again, the defender, lying on the ground, knocked the ball out of play with his hand, inside the penalty area. Kilmarnock made a concerted appeal for a penalty kick, but referee Mr Baillie apparently had not seen the hand used and gave a corner. After very strong appeals the referee consulted the linesman on that side and a penalty kick was then awarded. Amid the most intense excitement, gutsy little Benny Thomson stepped forward, and under immense pressure he drove the ball high into the net, just inside the post, to make it 3-3. Benny's colleagues mobbed him – it had been a nerve-racking moment but he was cool and just the right man for the job. It was anyone's game now. McPhail had the ball in the net, but a previous handling infringement meant it was ruled out. The teams took turns to launch attacks in the closing stages amid tremendous excitement and, just when most minds were turning to thoughts of a replay, a thunderbolt fell on Rangers. With two minutes to go, Ross, over on Killie's left, had the ball and he drove forward unchallenged and lofted it into Rangers' box, and from the ruck of players up rose Allan Collins, with shoulders hunched, to power a header past Dawson and set off scenes of wild excitement among the Killie fans.

Rangers desperately forced three corners in succession, but they were cleared and with play in midfield the referee signalled time up. The Kilmarnock players were mobbed as they made their way back to the pavilion after a famous victory, taking the club into its fifth Scottish Cup final.

The game was played in atrocious weather, and on pressure and scoring chances Rangers should have won, but they missed opportunities galore, while Kilmarnock, with their fantastic fighting spirit and ability to snap up what chances they made, had triumphed. Collins was Killie's best forward, with Thomson also playing excellently. McGrogan was enigmatic, but he had put in crosses for two goals. The Killie defence was sorely harassed at times, but Ross, Stewart and Hunter had done well. Fyfe and Milloy had a torrid time. Venters and Thornton had been the pick of the Rangers forwards, but fortunately Kinnear, Main and McPhail had off-days when it came to finishing. Brown in Rangers' midfield was an artist, and initiated most of their attacks; he was probably the classiest player of all and had not deserved to be in a losing side.

Two sad postscripts to this match followed for Kilmarnock. Despite having knocked out Celtic and Rangers (as well as local rivals Ayr United) on the way to the final, once there, the team rather ran out of steam. Having fallen behind with their fixtures, they faced a glut of matches at the end of the season and numerous injuries took their toll. In retrospect, trying to stick with the same group of players who had done so well was not the best policy, and an exhausted Killie team lost a replayed final 4-2 in extra time to Division Two East Fife. Incidentally, was this the first time that a club had beaten both members of the 'Old Firm' in both the League and the cup in one season? Both lost 2-1 in their League match at Rugby Park (at this time teams met only twice in the League each season). The other sad postscript concerns the scorer of two of Killie's goals, including the dramatic penalty kick equaliser. Two and a half years later Benny Thomson was dead, having lost his life when his ship, the SS *Balmare* was sunk by enemy action on 12 November 1940 when Benny was still only twenty-seven.

Queens Park v. Kilmarnock

Date: 14 January 1950   **Match title:** Scottish League B Division
Location: Hampden Park

Kilmarnock Football Club was certainly not unique in that it was badly hurt by the Second World War, but it would be fair to say that it suffered more than most football clubs. Having the ground requisitioned by the military in 1940 led to a complete shutdown until 1944, and even when they did restart, the damaged ground had been rendered unusable for a considerable period. In addition, with no games being played, they were unable to find and develop new talent. As a direct result the club was relegated from the top division at the end of the first official post-war season 1946/47, having been there since 1899. As money was strictly rationed, like so many other things in those days, times were very hard for Kilmarnock, and although the club was a big name in the lower division, a name did not win League points. Seasons 1947/48 and 1948/49 were hugely disappointing, as a multitude of players were tried and generally found wanting. Managers too had come and gone, and no perceptible improvement had taken place. By the dawn of the 1950s Killie were into their third season at the lower level and still toiling desperately to engineer their escape.

Season 1949/50 had started disastrously. From the first 6 League games only 2 points were accrued, and it seemed that promotion was further away than ever, but under manager Malky MacDonald the team suddenly perked up, and in the next 11 games only 1 was lost, 1 drawn and the other 9 won. The last of those games was a derby match against local rivals Ayr United on 2 January 1950, and Killie triumphed 4-0 in front of an excellent crowd of 23,520. Even though Killie lost at Tannadice the next day, the fans' spirits had been greatly lifted, and a new surge of enthusiasm embraced the club. When table-topping Morton came calling on the following Saturday 7 January, another fine attendance of 19,245 saw Killie win 2-0. The fans could finally see promotion on the horizon. So when a week later Kilmarnock faced a trip to Hampden to play Queens Park, many thousands of Killie fans travelled to Glasgow as the huge dormant Killie support had finally been roused.

The match turned out to be a feast of football for a crowd numbering 27,205, the highest attendance ever for a Scottish League match played outside of the top division. On ten minutes Kilmarnock forced a corner that Billy McKay lofted in and Tommy Johnston back-headed to Alex Donaldson, who first-timed a rocket-shot into the rigging. The amateurs might have had an equaliser from a penalty kick when Jimmy Hood brought down Boyd, but the wonderfully named referee Charles Faultless did not consider it worthy of a penalty. The play was hugely entertaining, with four wingers employed, and all four gave their respective full-backs a bit of a roasting at times. In the first half Queens Park's Boyd gave Killie's Hood an extremely difficult time, although Jimmy managed to keep him much quieter in the second half. The youthful Raymond Brown did the same with Ralph Collins, while conversely it was Killie's Billy McKay who gave Bob Gourlay the roasting in the second half, and Alex Donaldson did likewise with Queens Park's Stewart. It was in midfield that Kilmarnock had a definite advantage, with Doig and Middlemass giving their forwards a continual supply of the ball that their opponents could never equal. Twelve minutes into the second half McKay and Paton broke away on the

---

Queens Park 1
Grierson

Kilmarnock 3
Donaldson
Johnston, Cowan

The Kilmarnock eleven which played against Queens Park, although this picture was actually taken two weeks later before a cup tie against Stirling Albion. From left to right, back row: J. Brown (Trainer), J. Hood, R. Collins, J. Benson, R. Thyne, E. Doig, J. Middlemass. Front row: W. McKay, G. Paton, T. Johnston, S. Cowan, A. Donaldson.

right and Paton crossed for Johnston, a constant threat to Queens, to head a curling ball over Ronnie Simpson's upstretched arms. Two minutes later the score was pulled back to 2-1 when Grierson took advantage of a muddle in the Kilmarnock defence. Grierson, who should have scored in the first half when he headed wide with only Jimmy Benson to beat, should really also have equalised two minutes from time, when from what looked like an offside position he was allowed to go on, but he shot past the post. With the last kick of the game, Killie clinched this thriller. As the ball came into the goalmouth from a free-kick, the excellent Johnston, who later scored so many goals in England, headed it down to Sammy Cowan who promptly shot home, to give Killie a fine 3-1 win and Queens their first home League defeat of the season.

Both teams had played some great attacking football and the big crowd must have been delighted with the spectacle. Kilmarnock fully deserved to win, but it was a game full of incidents at both ends, and a credit to both teams. What's more, the trainers were never required on the field. Unfortunately after this thriller both teams rather fell away in the promotion race. Kilmarnock could only finish in seventh place and Queens ninth, so both were doomed to spend at least another season out of the elite. On their showing in this classic they were both capable of much better.

Queens Park: R. Simpson, T. Stewart, R. Galloway, A. Bell, G. Harbour, W. Hastie, A. Boyd, R. McKirdy, D. Grierson, G. Cunningham, R. Brown.
Kilmarnock: J. Benson, R. Collins, J. Hood, E. Doig, R. Thyne, J. Middlemass, W. McKay, G. Paton, T. Johnston, S. Cowan, A. Donaldson.

RANGERS v. KILMARNOCK

Date: 4 October 1952
Location: Hampden Park
Match title: Scottish League Cup Semi-Final

Season 1952/53 found Kilmarnock still stuck in B Division, and while it was true that Malky MacDonald had improved the quality of the playing staff, the reality was that they had lost 2 of the opening 3 League matches. On the other hand, they had performed well in the League Cup, which made up the opening fixtures of the season, and had won 7 of their 8 matches to find themselves in the semi-final, where old foes Rangers would be the opposition. Naturally Rangers, still able to field their famous 'Iron Curtain' defence, would be overwhelming favourites to defeat a B Division team.

The current Kilmarnock team had a problem in that while their forwards were extremely skilful, they were also very small, so perhaps playing against classier opposition would actually suit them better than taking on the more physical type of player they encountered in League games. Heneaghan, Harvey, Mays, Jack and Murray were all terrific ball-players, but was this enough?

The Kilmarnock players may have been nervous before the game but they quickly settled down to play a brand of football that undoubtedly surprised their opponents and most of the crowd. Experienced centre half Bob Thyne gave a performance of international standard (Bob had in fact played twice against England in wartime internationals) and he mastered Willie Thornton throughout. Behind him, goalkeeper John Niven was in magnificent form and never made a mistake (coincidentally, both 'keepers on the day were named Niven). With only eleven minutes gone, Derek Grierson had the ball in the Killie net, but it was clear that he had knocked it down with his hand, and referee J. Jackson of Glasgow did not allow the goal. Then Sammy Cox sent a long-range shot just past the post, but it was not all one-way as Harvey and Jack, with their quick darts and astute passes, gave the Rangers defence many worrying moments. They found they could open up the Rangers defence, but could not produce the killer touch to bring a goal, such as when Gerry Mays amazingly beat Willie Woodburn in the air and nodded down to Willie Jack, but Jack blazed it high over the bar. Thus, even though both sides had made some good chances, the teams turned around at 0-0.

Rangers, now playing against the wind, came out determined to stamp their authority on the match, and soon John Niven was forced to dive full length to parry a fine Grierson shot. For a spell it was all Rangers – Killie's Niven produced the save of the match by managing to touch away a Grierson header in miraculous fashion. He further distinguished himself by diving at the feet of first Hubbard and then Paton to avert danger. However, Kilmarnock weathered the storm, the defence never wilted and they came back into the game. George Young, who was given a torrid time by Matt Murray in the second half, headed the ball off the goal line after a Jack header had beaten the Rangers 'keeper, the second time that Young had been forced to perform this particular feat. With time running out and extra time beckoning, the ball was sent out to Murray on Killie's left wing and he again tricked his way past Young and left him behind. With the following wind billowing his shorts, he ran towards the Rangers goal, checked, and then slung a cross into the goalmouth. Niven and Johnny Little seemed to have the situation under control –

Rangers 0

Kilmarnock 1
Jack

Little controlled the ball a few yards from his own goal line and there was no danger, or so it appeared, until he looked up and saw Willie Jack racing towards him, so he thumped the ball away, but to his horror it struck the onrushing Jack and rebounded towards the goal, and slowly ran over the line. The Killie players jumped and danced with joy and the Ayrshire contingent in the crowd went crazy – with only one minute to go it was the winner.

It had been a hard-won and meritorious victory, even if the winning goal was a freak. As the underdogs, Killie had deserved it, even though Rangers had probably had more of the possession and chances. The Kilmarnock defence, particularly Niven and Thyne, had been immense and refused to yield despite Willie Waddell, Rangers' best attacker, proving such a handful. The small Killie forwards had shown themselves to be full of tricks, and Gerry Mays, despite his lack of inches, had repeatedly beaten Woodburn in the air. Clearly Kilmarnock was a B Division club playing A Division football.

Sadly, luck was not with Kilmarnock in the final. The team played well enough, but two late goals, scored by Bobby Flavell (who later joined Kilmarnock) gave Dundee a 2-0 victory.

Kilmarnock goalkeeper John Niven and full-back Ralph Collins thwart this Rangers attack.

Rangers: G. Niven, Young, Little, McColl, Woodburn, Cox, Waddell, Paton, Thornton, Grierson, Hubbard.

Kilmarnock: J. Niven, Collins, Hood, Russell, Thyne, Middlemass, Heneaghan, Harvey, Mays, Jack, Murray.

CELTIC v. KILMARNOCK

Date: 27 March 1957   **Match title:** Scottish Cup Semi-Final Replay
Location: Hampden Park

By 1957 Kilmarnock had become established in Division One, having finally achieved promotion back to the top in 1954 after seven seasons in Division B. They were not content with just surviving – they were actually challenging for third place and had reached the semi-finals of the Scottish Cup. On Saturday 23 March Kilmarnock played Celtic in their semi-final and 109,145 fans saw a 1-1 draw with Gerry Mays scoring for Killie and Celtic's John Higgins equalising eight minutes from time. The replay took place at Hampden on Wednesday 27 March 1957, before a disappointingly small crowd of 76,963. It was said that Celtic did not lose replays. This theory was about to be put to the test.

The return of Killie centre half Willie Toner was the only change to either side from the first game, and this certainly gave his team a boost. Toner was to be ice-cool throughout, and most people judged him the Man of the Match. Celtic were first to attack, but Killie 'keeper Jimmy Brown stopped a point-blank Higgins header with his feet after Alec Byrne had beaten Ralph Collins. Then for some reason Higgins and Collins swapped wings, Higgins going over to the left. The first half was fairly even until, on twenty-four minutes, Jack, harassed by Curlett, skied a clearance, and Celtic 'keeper Dick Beattie needlessly grabbed and pulled down Curlett as he tried to get to the ball as it came down. Referee Bobby Davidson of Airdrie had no hesitation in awarding a penalty kick. Mays struck the kick powerfully, Beattie dived to his left to block it, but Mays followed up to net the rebound. Kilmarnock played some delightful football, but it was Celtic who got an equaliser on thirty-five minutes. Bertie Peacock started the move, Byrne and Higgins quickly developed it and it ended with Bobby Collins netting from close range. This was Celtic's brightest spell, but they did not enjoy it for long – just eight minutes later Rab Stewart sent a perfect pass up the right wing to Curlett, who had switched positions with Mays, and as the ball came across from Curlett, eluding the defenders and the 'keeper, Gerry Mays coolly headed it home. Kilmarnock led 2-1 at the interval; they had been the superior team and had played much better than on the Saturday.

Celtic reshuffled their forward line at half-time, but Killie stayed on top for most of the second half and never looked in danger of defeat. Davie Burns just failed to connect with a Mays cross, and then in a Celtic break Brown kicked Fernie's shot off the line. It was Kilmarnock who increased their lead five minutes after half-time, when Mays sent Bertie Black through the middle with a perfect pass, but Bertie collided with goalkeeper Beattie. Both players stumbled, but Black was first to recover, and he pushed the ball with his right foot into the empty net. Little Bertie was without doubt the best forward on show in this match and his goal was well deserved. Playing now with supreme confidence they almost made it four, but Beattie just managed to get his hand to a powerful Mays shot. Celtic's only chances in the later stages came when, from Mochan's low shot, Brown instinctively raised his foot and for the third time in the game kicked clear, a bit of a speciality with the colourful Brown. Then Jimmy Stewart headed away from under the bar. Celtic showed all their traditional fight, but lacking the class of previous Celtic sides, relied

---

Celtic 1
Collins

Kilmarnock 3
Mays (2)
Black

mainly on power. Their best player was Bobby Evans, who ran himself ragged and only Collins and Fernie, despite the latter's tendency to lose possession, offered any threat to Killie. Mays had a late chance for his hat-trick but blazed over the bar with only the 'keeper to beat. When the final whistle sounded, Jimmy Brown threw his trademark red jockey cap high into the net and rushed out to hug Toner and skipper Collins. Jimmy had been criticised by some people for failing to cut out the corner kick that led to Celtic's late equaliser in the first match, but he atoned fully in the replay. Kilmarnock's great 3-1 victory was a triumph for teamwork. Brown, Toner, Rab Stewart, Black and Mays had been best, but all eleven played well. It would have been Celtic's fourth consecutive appearance in the cup final had they won, but it was Kilmarnock who went through to face a battling Falkirk team in the final. Sadly for Killie, after another 1-1 draw they were beaten 2-1 by the Bairns after extra time in a replay. Still, it had been a fine season for the Rugby Parkers – third place in the League behind Rangers and Hearts, and runners-up in the Scottish Cup gave the club a welcome financial boost.

Programme for the 1957 Scottish Cup semi-final. This was for the first match – no programme was issued for the replay.

Celtic: Beattie, Haughney, Fallon, Evans, Jack, Peacock, Higgins, Fernie, Byrne, Mochan, Collins.

Kilmarnock: Brown, Collins, J. Stewart, R. Stewart, Toner, Mackay, Mays, Harvey, Curlett, Black, Burns.

Rangers v. Kilmarnock

Date: 9 November 1957   **Match title:** Scottish League Division One
Location: Ibrox Park

This game was a seven-goal thriller at Ibrox, but the main talking point afterwards was the refereeing of Mr T.S. Edwards of Edinburgh. Both sides had grounds for complaint about his decisions, but perhaps Kilmarnock had more to complain about than Rangers.

Only five minutes into the game Kilmarnock took the lead when a corner from the right found Frank Beattie, and he got above 'keeper George Niven to head the ball down into the net. Killie almost had another soon after, but Niven managed to save Mays' shot with some difficulty. However, on fifteen minutes Rangers' Alex Scott beat Jim Stewart and passed to his South African colleague Don Kitchenbrand, who slipped the ball to another South African, Johnny Hubbard, and Hubbard struck a first-time shot to level the score. On thirty minutes Killie regained the lead. Bertie Black, who troubled Eric Caldow throughout, beat him with his customary tricky footwork and sent a perfect crossfield pass to Billy Muir. Muir returned it towards goal and Gerry Mays was there to turn the ball past Niven. Two minutes later it was 3-1 to the visitors when Mays headed on a Muir corner and Beattie blasted it into the corner of the net. Rangers tried to get back into the game but Brown produced a wonderful save from Billy Simpson's header. Then just before the interval came a ridiculous booking for Bertie Black, a cultured little ball-player to whom foul play was anathema. Bertie chased Caldow and managed to win the ball with a brilliant and certainly not illegal tackle, but to the surprise of friend and foe alike he was penalised, and when he tapped the ball away in disgust he was booked. Similarly, Simpson soon found himself booked for an innocuous tackle on Killie's Jim Stewart.

The Ibrox floodlights were switched on for the second half, and soon the referee was lecturing Sammy Baird and goalkeeper Jimmy Brown following a clash. A few minutes later Hubbard crossed and Kitchenbrand headed past Brown to reduce the deficit. Then came the major talking point of the match. Throughout the game Brown had been the victim of hefty charges by Kitchenbrand (not nicknamed 'The Rhino' for nothing), Baird and Simpson and the referee had turned a blind eye. Probably these charges were related to incidents in an earlier League Cup tie at Rugby Park. Nine minutes after half-time Simpson rushed Brown as he was making a clearance. The 'keeper, running out to clear with the ball in his hands and his arms held to his chest, bowled him over. The referee awarded a penalty to Rangers. Brown reacted furiously. In seconds jostling Killie players surrounded Mr Edwards and Willie Toner had to lead him out of the ruck of players. The decision stood and Hubbard made his usual immaculate job of the penalty kick. Killie had gone from 3-1 up to 3-3 within minutes and they were sore. The feeling was that the referee had allowed several illegal challenges on Brown when he was attempting to clear, but as soon as he gave the same back he was penalised.

At this time attitudes were changing, mainly through the realisation in Britain that the game was being played, and possibly played better, abroad. Charging 'keepers had been legal in the early days of soccer, but by this time it was dying out and was not generally done anymore. Kitchenbrand especially seemed like a throwback to earlier days – it was his speciality. Around six months later, what was probably the

---

Rangers 3
Hubbard (2, 1 pen)
Kitchenbrand

Kilmarnock 4
Beattie (2)
Mays, Curlett

Willie Toner and Gerry Mays displaying the very latest training gear in 1957.

death knell of the practice was sounded when Bolton's Nat Lofthouse charged Manchester United's Harry Gregg over the line in the 1958 FA Cup final. Most people were horrified that a referee could award a goal for what was really a minor assault (even Lofthouse admitted that he did not think a goal should have been awarded); today, he would be yellow-carded at least. Incidentally, it seems that the balance has swung too far the other way now, and 'keepers are over-protected.

For a time, losing their lead unnerved Killie's players, but they got over the bad spell, and in the fifty-eighth minute Rab Stewart lobbed a free-kick into Rangers' box and, surrounded by players, Niven could only palm the ball out as far as Davie Curlett, who sent a powerful header into the net for a spectacular winner. Although over half an hour remained, Kilmarnock had no great difficulty in keeping control of the rest of the match. They defended really well, but were by no means idle in attack. It was a well-merited victory. Mays had given centre half Moles an unhappy afternoon, and at the age of thirty-six he had scored his fourteenth goal of the season by early November in what was Killie's fourth win in the last five meetings of the clubs.

In fairness, it should be said that the referee had denied Rangers a second penalty kick, much more worthy than the one given, when Jim Stewart appeared to use both hands inside the box, but Mr Edwards either never saw or chose not to see that infringement, having already given Rangers one extremely doubtful penalty kick.

Rangers: Niven, Caldow, Little, McColl, Moles, Millar, Scott, Simpson, Kitchenbrand, Baird, Hubbard.
Kilmarnock: Brown, Collins, J. Stewart, R. Stewart, Toner, Kennedy, Muir, Curlett, Mays, Beattie, Black.

KILMARNOCK v. MOTHERWELL

Date: 27 February 1960   **Match title:** Scottish Cup Third Round
Location: Rugby Park

On the morning of Saturday 20 February 1960 Kilmarnock, with 10 consecutive victories behind them, lay third in the Scottish League, behind Hearts and Rangers, Rangers above Killie only on goal average. That day they were due to face Aberdeen at Pittodrie in a League match, but the weather put paid to the game, just as on the previous Saturday when Killie had been due to face Hearts at Tynecastle in the Scottish Cup second round. The cup tie was again postponed on the following Wednesday, 16 February and was not played until Monday 22 February, when in a thrilling match before 33,829 fans, Kilmarnock held Hearts to a 1-1 draw in Edinburgh. As the third round of the cup was due to take place on the next Saturday, Kilmarnock and Hearts were forced to replay just forty-eight hours later, and on Wednesday 24 February, another 24,359 enthralled fans saw a wonderful match in which Killie beat Hearts 2-1. Their reward was another cup tie, against a then very exciting and dangerous Motherwell team at Rugby Park on Saturday 27 February. Thus Killie played three cup ties on the Monday, Wednesday and Saturday, and all against formidable opposition. It was a very stiff test, but the team's fitness was considered one of its strongest assets, largely thanks to legendary trainer Walter W. McCrae.

29,412 fans turned up, the highest attendance ever at Rugby Park for a match that did not feature Celtic or Rangers as the opposition. In the first half Motherwell's defence, not considered the strongest part of their team, held the in-form Killie attack, cleverly led by Andy Kerr. At times the home side hammered 'Well, forcing around a dozen corners in the first twenty minutes or so. Kerr came close with an overhead kick but Mackin held it; Andy also sliced a shot wide from good position. Then Jackie McInally dallied when a chance presented itself, but the worst miss came when Billy Muir drove the ball across the face of an empty goal. A penalty-kick claim was turned down when Martis was thought to have handled when Muir tried to knock the ball over his head. By way of reply, Motherwell only had three corners and one real chance in the first half when Ian St John nearly netted a header from an Andy Weir cross which deceived Jimmy Brown. Despite all Kilmarnock's pressure, the teams went in at the interval goal-less.

Motherwell, who now had the wind at their backs and must have been the fresher team given that this was Kilmarnock's third tough cup tie inside six days, came out fighting at the start of the second half. Willie Hunter beat Matt Watson at the byline and whipped over a cross that went just wide of the post. However, on fifty-five minutes came the breakthrough. Kerr crossed from the left, Reid and Mackin got in each other's way and McInally nipped in to push the ball over the line. Ten minutes later the game was as good as over. Bertie Black initially lost the ball but recovered to win it back. He then rounded two defenders and slipped it to Kerr. Andy's fierce shot struck a post, ran along the line, hit the other post and in came that man McInally to again knock it home. Kilmarnock now decided it was time to close-up shop and allow Motherwell to come at them. The visitors managed to force numerous corners, but it was all to no avail, as the Killie defence was an impenetrable wall. This was a Motherwell team containing no less than six men

---

Kilmarnock 2   **Motherwell 0**
McInally (2)

who either had, or would in the near future have full international caps for Scotland. McPhee came nearest to scoring with a fine effort which Brown pushed over the bar, but they were showing only occasional flashes of their famed skills. Their best spell was the last ten minutes after Hunter and McPhee swapped positions, but Killie's defenders thwarted their scoring attempts and although extremely tired they were happy to find themselves in the quarter-final of the Scottish Cup when the final whistle came. Willie Toner had given a faultless display and had completely mastered the highly rated, but on this day frustrated, St John (later to find further fame at Liverpool). Kerr up front had given Martis a very uncomfortable time, but it was in the midfield that Killie had been most dominant through Frank Beattie and Bobby Kennedy. This was their thirteenth match without defeat and the run was to continue. Between 5 December 1959, when Killie lost at Ibrox, and 2 April 1960, when they beat Clyde in the cup semi-final, Kilmarnock played 21 League and Scottish Cup matches, winning 20 and drawing 1 (the cup tie at Tynecastle). Unfortunately a poor start in the league handicapped them, and Killie could only finish second behind Hearts in the League and they then lost 2-0 to Rangers in the Scottish Cup final. Nevertheless, it was a fine season.

Motherwell's Ian St John cannot quite get his header on target as Jimmy Brown and Willie Toner are caught out.

Kilmarnock: Brown, Richmond, Watson, Beattie, Toner, Kennedy, R. Stewart, McInally, Kerr, Black, Muir.

Motherwell: Mackin, McSeveney, Reid, Aitken, Martis, McCann, Hunter, Quinn, St John, McPhee, Weir.

KILMARNOCK v. BURNLEY

Date: 1 June 1960   **Match title:** International Soccer League Tournament
Location: Polo Grounds, New York

The president of the New York Americans soccer team, William D. Cox, realised a dream when he managed, after two years of planning, to organise a major international soccer tournament in the USA. Twelve top teams, from different countries, ten European, one Brazilian and a composite American team (many of them born in Britain) competed against each other in two six-team sections, and the two section winners were to play for the 'American Challenge Cup'.

Kilmarnock, runners-up in the Scottish League, represented Scotland, and the other five teams in the section comprised Nice (France), Bayern Munich (West Germany), Glenavon (Northern Ireland), the New York Americans select team and Burnley, who had just won the League Championship in England. In Killie's first game they beat Bayern Munich 3-1, coming back from one down at half-time, and in the second match they fairly comfortably defeated Glenavon 2-0. The third match was the most eagerly awaited, as the opposition was Burnley and a real Scotland v. England battle was anticipated. It has to be said that Burnley had not particularly endeared themselves to either their American hosts or the other teams in the group. Kilmarnock, Bayern and Glenavon had all flown to America together from Prestwick Airport and shared the same hotels, and many friendships had been

Programme for the Burnley v. Kilmarnock game in the USA.

Kilmarnock 2
Kerr
Wentzel

        Burnley 0

made between the rival players, but Burnley kept themselves apart from all the others and had found continual cause for complaint about the hotel service, match and travel arrangements and so on. Indeed, they walked out of the George Hotel, which all the other clubs had found to be quite satisfactory.

1 June 1960 was a typically hot, steamy New York evening when the game kicked off. Burnley and Kilmarnock were now the favourites, and this game would go a long way to deciding who topped the section. It turned out to be a tough, bad-tempered contest, like a cup tie with vigorous tackling and fast action, despite the heat. English referee Dennis Howell (a Labour MP and future Minister of Sport) had a difficult job on his hands. With eighteen minutes gone Kilmarnock took the lead when that prodigious goalscorer Andy Kerr received the ball from Tommy Bryceland, met it on the turn and, despite being harassed by Cummings, cracked a beauty past Burnley goalkeeper Adam Blacklaw, a future Scottish international. Bryceland had replaced Bertie Black, victim of a double fracture of the cheekbone in an Ayrshire Cup match against Ayr United, on the trip. On twenty-six minutes Kerr netted a splendid individual effort, but it was disallowed and a free-kick given against Kerr. The Scots in the crowd voiced their displeasure very loudly at this point as no infringement had been apparent. Burnley, for all their polished attacking play and a team containing no less than seven players who either had, or would in the future gain full international caps, could do little to offer a real threat to the Killie goal. Willie Toner at centre half rarely let the highly rated Ray Pointer (soon to play for England) have a look in, while Bobby Kennedy (transferred to Manchester City for £45,000 a year later) saw to it that Irish international Jimmy McIlroy, probably the best player in his position in Britain at the time, was not allowed to demonstrate his undoubted talents. They could not find a weakness in the Killie defence, and became more and more frustrated as the game went on. The 13,000 fans witnessed a thriller and, just a minute before the end, Kilmarnock crowned their victory with a second goal from Vernon Wentzel following a free-kick. Burnley were irate at the finish – their manager Harry Potts had to be warned by referee Howell during the game when he had risen from his seat to abuse one of the Killie players, and after the match further protests led to Mr Howell forwarding a report to the USFA and the FA in England regarding comments made to him by Burnley officials. A war of words broke out between the two camps over the following days, and Burnley's famously outspoken chairman Bob Lord was at the centre of it with some typically provocative statements. One well-known English writer, however, declared that Burnley had let the side down with their tantrums and that their behaviour was a bad advertisement for English football.

In the end it was irrelevant. Burnley had greatly underestimated the opposition. Killie won 2-0 and they followed up by drawing 1-1 with Nice and beating the New York Americans 3-1. Kilmarnock thus topped the first section of the tournament with 9 points, winning 4 and drawing 1 of their 5 matches. The team returned home to allow the second section to be played, and this was won by Brazilians Bangu. Killie then had to fly back to New York to face Bangu on 6 August for the 'American Challenge Cup' to be awarded to the overall winners. An excellent Bangu team won this final match deservedly 2-0.

Kilmarnock: Brown, Richmond, Watson, Beattie, Toner, Kennedy, Wentzel, McInally, Kerr, Bryceland, Muir.

Burnley: Blacklaw, Angus, Elder, Adamson, Cummings, Miller, Meredith, McIlroy, Pointer, Robson, Pilkington.

RANGERS v. KILMARNOCK

Date: 26 November 1960   **Match title:** Scottish League Division One
Location: Ibrox Park

50,000 fans turned up at Ibrox for a meeting of the top two teams in the League. The champions of the previous season, Hearts, had made a very poor start to the season and could already be discounted from the championship race. Even this early in the season it was clear that only Kilmarnock, runners-up in 1959/60, could stop an outstanding Rangers team from regaining the title.

Early on Killie found they were being pushed back into defence by a sweet-moving Rangers team inspired by the brilliant twenty-one-year-old sensation Jim Baxter, recently signed from Raith Rovers, and the somewhat older, but equally skilful, Ian McMillan. Killie's inspirational half-back Frank Beattie had been forced out of this vital match by tonsillitis, and with young goalkeeper Sandy McLaughlan making only his third first-team appearance they seemed to be right up against it.

It looked like another blow to Killie when full-back Jim Richmond headed away an Alex Scott piledriver that would have opened the scoring and was knocked unconscious, but he recovered after a short spell. Then, on just fourteen minutes Rangers took the lead. Scott raced away after clever play by Baxter and McMillan, crossed the ball, Millar headed it on to Davie Wilson and he struck it home via McLaughlan's legs. Things were not looking good for the visitors at this stage. However, Killie tried to hit back immediately and were unlucky when, from Bobby Kennedy's cross, Andy Kerr's header beat George Niven but smacked off the bar. Then McLaughlan dropped a Wilson shot and with an open goal to shoot at McMillan sliced the ball wide from only five yards. The Rangers fans soon forgave his miss however, for on thirty-five minutes the ball was headed back out to him following a corner kick, and McMillan coolly killed the ball and gave McLaughlan no chance with a shot into the top corner. Rangers were now 2-0 up and coasting, apparently!

Five minutes after Rangers' second goal, the fightback began when Jackie McInally met a Billy Muir cross deflected to him by Harold Davis, and calmly side-footed the ball past Niven. Two minutes later Kennedy sent Bertie Black away on the right and when his cross came in Andy Kerr was on the spot to knock it high into the net from just a few yards out. The half-time whistle saw a stunned Rangers team go in at 2-2 and the game had been transformed.

On the resumption Kilmarnock switched Brown and Black. Hugh Brown seemed to revel in the extra freedom he got on the right wing and showed off his clever ball skills. Indeed Baxter, who had fallen out of the game after his sparkling play early on, was warned by referee Hugh Phillips following a bad foul on Brown. The right-winger had possibly the best forty-five minutes of his Killie career in the second-half. He rounded Eric Caldow and cut the ball back to Kerr, who would normally have been expected to score, but on this occasion Andy drove it over the bar. Then Brown forced Niven to scramble across his goal to push his shot away for a corner, but he would not be denied and with only five minutes left, Hugh collected a fine pass from McInally and with the Rangers defenders retreating, anticipating a pass to a colleague, he surprised them by releasing a low shot from just outside the penalty area. The ball whizzed past Niven into the corner of the net to clinch an amazing 3-2 victory from a seemingly hopeless position earlier in the game.

Rangers 2
Wilson
McMillan

Kilmarnock 3
McInally, Kerr
H. Brown

Rangers, hot favourites for the League Championship and fielding eight players who gained full international caps for Scotland, had been defeated in front of their own fans, and the League title race was now a real contest after all. If Hugh Brown could lay claim to be the match-winner, Willie Toner at centre half for Kilmarnock could be said to have been the match-saver. Willie was again superb, showing himself to be ice-cool under pressure and an inspiring captain. Clearly had Toner been with a more fashionable club he would have played far more than a miserly two games for Scotland. The whole team had shown guts and sound teamwork to pull off this glorious victory, coping by improvising against a Rangers side that had displayed artistry in the early stages of the match and had then produced powerful play in the later stages when they staged a desperate rally trying to force an equaliser.

The 1960/61 Scottish League Championship race went right to the final day. It was a two-horse race, but in the end Rangers held on, beating already-relegated Ayr United 7-3 in the last game of the season to take the title with 51 points to Killie's 50.

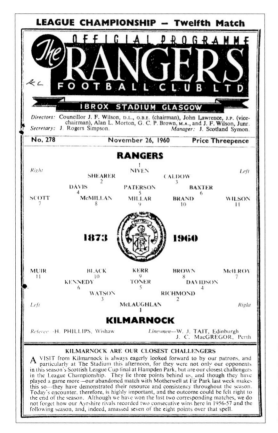

Match programme for Killie's remarkable 3-2 win at Ibrox, where they came back from two goals down. Rangers' team was unchanged from that shown on the front of the programme. Kilmarnock made a slight change to their forward line.

Rangers: Niven, Shearer, Caldow, Davis, Paterson, Baxter, Scott, McMillan, Millar, Brand, Wilson.

Kilmarnock: McLaughlan, Richmond, Watson, Davidson, Toner, Kennedy, Black, H. Brown, Kerr, McInally, Muir.

KILMARNOCK v. AIRDRIE

Date: 29 September 1962   **Match title:** Scottish League Division One
Location: Rugby Park

Kilmarnock made a devastating start to the 1962/63 season. As was traditional then the season began with League Cup sectional fixtures. They swept through to the semi-final, playing 8 matches, winning 7 and drawing 1, scoring 25 goals along the way. However League matches had proved a little trickier as Killie had won only 1 of the first 4, and some of the harder-to-please fans were unhappy, believing that they had already given their rivals for the Championship a head start. The fifth League game of the season was at home against Airdrie, who had beaten Raith Rovers 8-1 the previous Saturday.

A disappointing crowd of only 7,317 turned up, but they were soon rewarded with an opening goal by the home side in only five minutes. Clever little scheming inside forward Davie Sneddon, signed from Preston a year before, combined with big Frank Beattie to create an opening for Andy Kerr to smash a rocket-shot past the helpless Airdrie goalkeeper Jim Samson. Just seven minutes later Samson was again in action – this time he pulled down Bertie Black and Kerr made his usual expert job of converting the resultant penalty kick. Kerr then completed the remarkable feat of scoring a hat-trick in the first fifteen minutes when Sneddon again set him up and Andy sent another raging shot into the net, giving the unfortunate Samson no chance. Airdrie were simply unable to cope with a rampaging Kilmarnock team who had struck form and were playing with power and precision. For a brief spell at 3-0 Airdrie did have a short flirtation with the Kilmarnock goal area, but the Killie onslaught returned all too soon for them and on thirty-two minutes the score increased to 4-0. O'Connor's shot, which might actually have gone wide, was deflected off Airdrie defender McNeil and Samson was again stranded. The home fans had only to wait two more minutes for the next goal. Sneddon fastened onto a Kerr pass (reversing the normal routine for once) and Davie scored a smartly taken fifth goal. Samson was being kept very busy, while Sandy McLaughlan in the Killie goal was a virtual spectator, his only testing moment of the first half coming when Rowan hit a ferocious shot and Sandy was forced into a brilliant save. Killie's Brien McIlroy had to go off five minutes before half-time with blood streaming from a nasty eye gash. His team-mates managed to hold on to their 5-0 lead until the interval.

McIlroy was back in place, having received four stitches to his wound, at the second half kick-off. Demoralised Airdrie found themselves pushed back into defence against constant Killie pressure. Samson had good saves from Kerr and Black, but on sixty minutes he was beaten again when the astute Kerr dummied a McIlroy cross to leave Pat O'Connor a clear view of goal. Pat, who at the time was doing his National Service and was being flown back from Germany on a weekly basis to play for Kilmarnock, made no mistake and shot his team into a 6-0 lead. Killie should then have been awarded a second penalty kick when Black was blatantly pushed, but perhaps referee A. Crossman of Edinburgh felt some sympathy for the visitors and turned away the claims. Then Sneddon ought to have scored his second when he dribbled through but sliced a close-range shot wide of the mark. Then it was Beattie's turn to come forward and send a powerful shot over the bar.

Kilmarnock 8   **Airdrie 0**
Kerr (5, 1 pen)
O'Connor (2)
Sneddon

'Handy Andy' Kerr, scorer of five goals in the game against Airdrie.

Ten minutes from the end Kerr netted his fourth and Kilmarnock's seventh when he coolly lofted an O'Connor cross into the net. Three minutes from time Andy did it again – this time a Jim Richmond lob into the goal area provided the opportunity for 'Handy Andy' to strike his fifth goal, sending another immaculate shot home to complete the scoring at 8-0. Airdrie had been thoroughly outplayed – Killie were vastly superior and, but for Samson, the score could easily have been into double figures. Kerr had scored five and had a part in all three of the others with his crafty play.

These goals took Andy to the top of Scottish Division One scoring charts for the season. He now had 16 goals in League and League Cup matches, putting him 2 ahead of Rangers' Jimmy Millar. He was a veritable goal-machine, his coolness in front of goal legendary. He was also a laid-back character and much loved by the fans, who were saddened by Kilmarnock's acceptance of a £25,000 offer by Sunderland for his transfer the following March, by which time he had 35 goals for the season. The club could justifiably claim that this was an excellent offer for a player who was approaching his thirty-second birthday, and possibly the transfer came too late in his career for Andy himself, but how would Killie ever replace his near goal-a-game record over the three and a half years he spent thrilling the fans at Rugby Park? Some people would argue that the club has never managed to find such a natural goalscorer since.

Kilmarnock: McLaughlan, Richmond, Watson, O'Connor, McGrory, Beattie, H. Brown, Black, Kerr, Sneddon, McIlroy.

Airdrie: Samson, Jonquin, Keenan, McNeil, Hannah, Thomson, Murray, Rowan, Tees, Duncan, Coats.

Rangers v. Kilmarnock

Date: 10 October 1962
Location: Hampden Park

Match title: League Cup Semi-Final

Kilmarnock went into this match determined to avenge their defeats by Rangers in the Scottish Cup final of 1960 and the League Cup final of the following season. The players were tired of coming close in all three major competitions without actually winning anything.

The team settled quickly in this semi-final before 76,043 fans and took the lead with only sixteen minutes played. A Brien McIlroy shot was headed away by Eric Caldow straight to Hugh Brown, who immediately returned it to McIlroy to beat 'keeper Billy Ritchie with a neat header. Unfortunately for Killie the lead was to last for only three minutes, Rangers hitting back with a goal from Ralph Brand, whose long-range effort seemed to be deflected past goalkeeper McLaughlan by Matt Watson. Brand did it again with just another three minutes gone, giving a pass to Davie Wilson and running into position to take the return and stick it in the Killie net to put Rangers ahead 2-1. Kilmarnock then took another serious blow when full-back Watson injured a leg in a tackle and had to move to outside left with Davie Sneddon going to left-back. This was, of course, in the days before substitutes, and the limping Watson was given the role of acting as a mere nuisance to Rangers on the left wing. It has to be said that Sneddon made an excellent job of his unfamiliar defensive role, and he kept Rangers' dangerous Scottish international winger Willie Henderson in check admirably. It might have been 3-1 to Rangers when a John Greig shot looked to be a scorer until Brand got in the way. He appeared to be in an offside position and also to handle the ball as well before putting it in the net; referee Bobby Davidson of Airdrie had no doubts and ruled out the goal. As if to celebrate this escape Killie raced up the field and scored a well-taken equaliser. The ball went from Sneddon to Beattie, Beattie to Black and then a magnificent Black pass played inside Rangers defender Ronnie McKinnon to Andy Kerr set him up perfectly to level the score at 2-2 at the interval.

The second half proved to be a hectic, end-to-end, furiously fought battle. The Kilmarnock midfielders were excelling; O'Connor and Beattie began to take charge and Beattie's performance in this game put the legendary Jim Baxter in the shade. Indeed, Baxter blotted his copybook and had his name taken for a rough tackle on O'Connor. Young Jackie McGrory at centre half was also magnificent, and showed himself to be a worthy successor to Willie Toner, keeping Jimmy Millar quiet. Watson returned to his normal left-back position, and though far from fit, managed to hold his own against the tricky Henderson. Sandy McLaughlan was superb when he had to be, but in truth that was not all that often thanks to those in front of him. The Rangers defence was not as well-balanced or as close-knit as Kilmarnock's as both sides fought for the winning goal and the excitement mounted. Ritchie had to pull off a magnificent save from Sneddon, and then at the other end McLaughlan equalled it with a masterly save from a Wilson effort. The injured Watson managed to clear a Harold Davis header off the line. Then Hugh Brown had a thrilling run, but spoiled it with a weak finish. Then joy for Killie, as with ten minutes left they won a corner and as Sneddon's kick came across little Bertie Black headed it back over his shoulder into the net, Caldow's despairing attempt to keep it out

Rangers 2	Kilmarnock 3
Brand (2)	*McIlroy*
	Kerr, Black

succeeding only in helping it on its way. It was a long last ten minutes for the Killie players and fans as Rangers made desperate but unavailing efforts to save the game. In the last minute McIlroy broke away and should have made the score 4-2, but clear with only Ritchie to beat, he muffed this great chance by shooting into the side-netting. It did not matter too much as the final whistle sounded immediately after and Kilmarnock had made it into the League Cup final.

The final though was to be yet another disappointment for Kilmarnock, who were rapidly gaining the title of 'champion runners-up'. They lost 1-0 to a Norrie Davidson goal for Hearts, and had the extra disappointment of having an equalising 'goal' from Frank Beattie disallowed by referee Tom Wharton in the last minute, supposedly for handball. As well as that, Kilmarnock ended the 1962/63 season runners-up to Rangers in the League again.

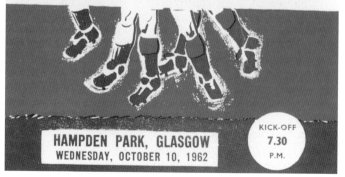

Match programme for Killie's victorious League Cup semi-final of 1962. The sketch on the front cover was used on several other big match programmes in that era.

Rangers: Ritchie, Shearer, Caldow, Davis, McKinnon, Baxter, Henderson, Greig, Millar, Brand, Wilson.

Kilmarnock: McLaughlan, Richmond, Watson, O'Connor, McGrory, Beattie, H. Brown, Black, Kerr, Sneddon, McIlroy.

KILMARNOCK v. CELTIC

Date: 27 March 1963   **Match title:** Scottish League Division One
Location: Rugby Park

On Wednesday 27 March 1963 Celtic visited Rugby Park for a floodlit League match. Like hundreds of other matches during that most memorable season, the game had been postponed earlier due to the abnormally bad weather that had seen snow and ice cause havoc throughout Britain for fully three months. So severe had been the winter that this season saw the initiation of the Pools Panel to decide on the outcome of postponed games, as the Pools companies could no longer tolerate the loss of business that postponements created. This match had originally been scheduled for 2 February, and given the eventual outcome Celtic must have dearly wished that it had taken place on the original date. Both teams were below their full strength for this contest. Goalkeeper McLaughlan was a late call-off and McInally and McIlroy were also absentees from the forwards. In addition Pat O'Connor, still doing his National Service in Germany, was unavailable for midweek games. Eric Murray stood in for O'Connor and Campbell Forsyth played in goal for Killie for only the third time that season and only the seventh time in all. Celtic had a goalkeeping problem of their own and Dick Madden came in for his debut. Another debutant for Celtic was an extremely promising young right-winger called Jimmy Johnstone, of whom a great deal more would later be heard! In addition Billy McNeil was unavailable and the muscular multilinguist John Cushley was Billy's replacement. Just over 16,000 fans were present that evening to see the teams sitting in second place (Killie) and fourth place (Celtic) in the League play, with a very strong Rangers team at the top. Kilmarnock welcomed Mr Bill Cox of the International Soccer League, based in the USA, who had arrived that day and was there to finalise the selection of the Scottish representative for the 1963 summer League tournament. It was to be Kilmarnock, just as it had been in 1960 and 1961.

Kilmarnock dominated the match from the start. Black and Mason missed good early chances, but then with only nine minutes gone they took the lead when 'keeper Madden misjudged a Davie Sneddon free-kick and could only palm it down to Joe Mason's feet for Joe to knock home. Inspired by the intelligent play of Kerr, Sneddon and Black, Killie created havoc in the Celts defence, and with Black's darting runs and Sneddon's delightful passing it was only a matter of time until a second goal was scored. It came on thirty-one minutes when, following a smart Andy Kerr pass, Sneddon hit a twenty-yard shot past Madden. Kerr was proving to be too crafty for the inexperienced Cushley, while experienced midfielders Duncan McKay and Billy Price could not subdue their opposite numbers. The score remained at 2-0 until half-time, but within six minutes of the restart Killie had doubled their tally. On forty-six minutes Black was allowed a free shot which he did not pass up, and on fifty-one minutes Kerr netted from a penalty kick. With fifty-seven minutes played it was 5-0 as Kerr set up Black and Bertie put away his second goal of the evening. Celtic briefly rallied at this point as they tried to pull at least one goal back, but it was in vain. Bobby Craig and Charlie Gallagher (a former Kilmarnock Amateurs player) were far too busy trying to assist their overworked defence to create any real chances. Davie Sneddon was the best player on the field, even if his subtle skills were not always fully appreciated by the home fans. He found gaps and fully exploited them with his

---

Kilmarnock 6   **Celtic 0**
Mason, Sneddon
Black (2)
Kerr (2, 1 pen)

Campbell Forsyth in training. He was capped 4 times by Scotland while with Kilmarnock and kept a clean sheet against Celtic.

delicate chips and lobs, but he also found time to assist back in defence when it was required. Ten minutes from the end Kerr finished the scoring after Sneddon and Mason had done the lead-up work. It was Kerr's thirty-fifth goal of the season. Little did the Killie fans realise at the time that this was to be Andy's last goal for the club – within days he was transferred to Sunderland. It was his 113th goal in 137 competitive games for Killie. It was also a remarkably good way to sign off, in a 6-0 win over Celtic.

Modern-day fans may look at this result and consider it a one-off fluke. However, it should be pointed out that Kilmarnock scored 92 League goals that season, and at that time Division One was an eighteen-team League with teams only playing each other once at home and once away per season. In the next two seasons, 1963/64 and 1964/65, Celtic would lose 4-0 and 5-2 in their League encounters at Rugby Park.

Kilmarnock: Forsyth, Richmond, Watson, Murray, McGrory, Beattie, H. Brown, Mason, Kerr, Sneddon, Black.
Celtic: Madden, Young, Kennedy, McKay, Cushley, Price, Johnstone, Craig, Chalmers, Gallagher, F. Brogan.

KILMARNOCK v. FALKIRK

Date: 8 February 1964   **Match title:** Scottish League Division One
Location: Rugby Park

On Saturday 1 February 1964 Kilmarnock suffered a surprise 2-0 defeat against Partick Thistle at Firhill. This defeat knocked Killie off the top of the League after a six-week stay, and allowed Rangers to take a single-point lead over them. Accusations of complacency were made against some of the players. So, when Falkirk came calling the following Saturday the Rugby Parkers were determined to regain both their pride and their place at the top.

With only one minute gone, Killie looked well on the way to restoring their fans' faith. Young full-back Stuart Layburn, in for the injured Andy King, found winger Brien McIlroy with a long pass, and McIlroy crashed a right-foot shot into the net. Just three minutes later Falkirk's goalkeeper Willie Whigham could not hold another McIlroy shot and Frank Beattie was on hand to knock the rebound in for a second goal and a wonderful start for the home side. With nineteen minutes played a neat interpassing move between Jackie McInally and Hugh Brown was completed by a shot from the former, and the Bairns found themselves down 3-0. On twenty-nine minutes McIlroy made the opening for McInally to score his second and Killie's fourth, and just three minutes after that the same man completed a hat-trick in thirteen minutes, following a magnificent solo run right through the defence and a dribble round Whigham. Jackie McInally was a hero to the Kilmarnock supporters, but he could be an inconsistent player, capable of the most exquisite runs and shots showing both power and grace, but also capable on his off-days of missing easier chances. Jackie (father of Alan McInally of Celtic, Aston Villa, Bayern Munich and Scotland among others) rarely scored ordinary goals and this effort for his hat-trick resembled a number of others scored during his career. In fact, whenever the author thinks of Big Jackie it immediately brings to mind an image of him running from the halfway line beating man after man and finishing by going round the goalkeeper and putting the ball in the net.

With forty-four minutes on the clock Killie scored an amazing goal. Davie Sneddon took a short corner to Beattie, who passed it back to McIlroy for the winger to beat Whigham from an almost impossible position on the byline to make the half-time score 6-0. With just two minutes gone in the second half, Sneddon fired over a cross that the 'keeper could only parry, and Hugh Brown was on the spot to first-time it over the line. With fifty minutes gone it became 8-0, with McIlroy becoming the second Killie hat-trick man of the game when he scored after fastening onto an Eric Murray pass. Four more minutes and the total moved up to nine. McIlroy outpaced Ian Rae and hammered an unsaveable shot past Whigham. By now the home fans, or at least those familiar with football record books, might have been thinking of their team creating a new Scottish League record victory for the top division. It was then, and still is today, the 11-0 Celtic win over Dundee in 1895. With thirty-six minutes still left this record looked well within Killie's grasp. Even though Davie Sneddon had been injured in a tackle by Jim Pierson (for which Pierson became the only booking of the game by referee R. Rodger of Stenhouse), and was having to play out on the left wing, he was still an influence on the game as his team dominated with their brilliant blend of power and pace. In the sixty-first

---

Kilmarnock 9   **Falkirk 2**
McIlroy (4)   *Maxwell (2)*
McInally (3)
Beattie, Brown

minute Killie were awarded a penalty kick when Pierson pulled down McInally. What a situation, almost half an hour to go and a penalty kick to go 10-0 up! However, McIlroy's kick was a weak one and Whigham saved easily. It would have been the little winger's fifth goal of the match. Within a minute Falkirk had gone down to the other end and Hugh Maxwell (signed by Celtic nine months later) shot home. Kilmarnock had relaxed and lost some of their momentum. McIlroy and Beattie both passed up good chances to score, and then with eighty minutes gone Maxwell headed another Falkirk goal from a Willie Fulton free-kick. The game finished in a convincing 9-2 victory for Kilmarnock. It could have been a record score, but on the other hand Falkirk had not performed nearly as badly as the score suggests. It was just that Killie's outstanding teamwork, with every player contributing, was just too much for the Bairns. Beattie, McIlroy (a winger whose goals tally for the season was now 23), McInally and Sneddon until his injury, were the outstanding players. As it turned out, Kilmarnock were the only home team to win in the nine Division One matches played that day. With Rangers losing to St Mirren, the Rugby Park outfit were back at the top of the League by a point. Unfortunately, Killie did not manage to stay top and finished the season in second place for the fourth time in five years.

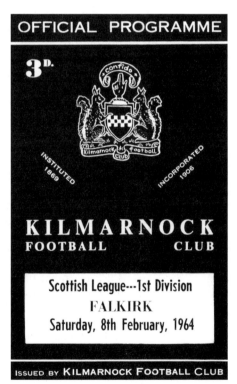

Left: Programme for the match v. Falkirk. *Above:* Brien McIlroy, who scored four goals against Falkirk in the 9-2 win (and he missed a penalty kick!).

Kilmarnock: Forsyth, Layburn, Watson, McFadzean, McGrory, Beattie, H. Brown, McInally, Murray, Sneddon, McIlroy.
Falkirk: Whigham, Thomson, Hunter, Pierson, Rae, Fulton, Redpath, Davidson, Wilson, Maxwell, Gourlay.

KILMARNOCK v. EINTRACHT FRANKFURT

Date: 22 September 1964
Location: Rugby Park

Match title: Fairs Cities Cup First Round, Second Leg

Playing in front of around 20,000 German fans in Frankfurt on Wednesday 2 September 1964, Kilmarnock had disappointingly gone down 3-0 in the first leg of their Fairs Cup (now called the UEFA Cup) tie. Killie's newly developed 4-4-2 system, which manager Willie Waddell was sure was the way forward, had not worked as well as expected and despite holding the Germans to 0-0 at half-time, two quick goals just after the break, on fifty-three and fifty-four minutes, and another later had left the Rugby Park team with a mountain to climb in the second leg. Eintracht, founded as far back as 1899, were considered one of Europe's top teams, and Scottish fans in particular held their name in reverence in view of their part in what many people still consider the finest game of football ever played. The European Cup final of 1960 at Hampden between Real Madrid and Eintracht was a ten-goal classic, and although the Germans had been beaten 7-3 they performed well – it was just that they were facing an eleven that was rated Real's greatest ever, including Alfredo Di Stefano, Ferenc Puskas and Francisco Gento. It was widely believed that Eintracht would have beaten any side other than Real that day; after all, they had beaten a strong Rangers team by 6-1 at home and 6-3 at Ibrox in the two legs of the 1960 semi-final. So impressive had they been in their visits to Glasgow that Eintracht were invited to come back to play Rangers again in the match to officially open the floodlights at Hampden Park in 1961, and they defeated Rangers again 3-2. Such was the pedigree of the Germans that most people gave Kilmarnock very little chance of getting through to the next round, especially after the result in the first leg. Five of the players from the 1960 final took part in the match in Germany.

What Kilmarnock really wanted in the second-leg match at Rugby Park was an early goal to eat into the three-goal deficit, and an early goal is just what the game produced. Unfortunately it was not for the home side! With only two minutes gone Huberts drove through the middle and cracked a magnificent twenty-yard shot past Campbell Forsyth to put Killie 4-0 down on aggregate, and the already slim chance of victory seemed to have gone completely. The home fans were shocked, but not the players. Against such renowned opponents this should have knocked the heart out of them, but it appeared to have the opposite effect and spurred Kilmarnock on to tremendous effect. Egon Loy in goal for Eintracht produced fine saves from McIlroy and Sneddon, but was beaten on twelve minutes when Davie Sneddon pushed the ball left to Jackie McInally, Jackie crossed it into the box where it was deflected off the arm of Weber, and as some fans were roaring for a penalty kick it fell at the left foot of young Ronnie Hamilton and he knocked it high into the net. With seventeen minutes gone Killie took a lead on the night. Eric Murray passed the ball to Andy King, Andy made ground down the right wing and played it to Frank Beattie inside the Germans' box. Frank pushed it back out to Tommy McLean, and as Tommy's low cross came in, eluding defender Blusch, Brien McIlroy, goal-snatcher supreme, was there to hit it low past Loy. Kilmarnock continued to dominate the game until the interval but could not improve on their 2-1 lead before referee J. Adair from Belfast blew for half-time.

Kilmarnock 5
Hamilton (2), McIlroy
McFadzean, McInally

Eintrach Frankfurt 1
Huberts

Eintracht came out more determined for the second half, and in the early stages looked to have pulled themselves together again and produced one or two attacking movements, but it did not last long and soon they found they were being swamped by Killie's unremitting attacks, driven on by a frenzied crowd. Ten minutes into the second half the classy and greatly underrated Jim McFadzean moved upfield as a Jackie McGrory free-kick, taken from just inside the visitors' half, was floated into the penalty area. The tall figure of McFadzean got his head to it and glanced the ball low inside the right-hand corner of Loy's net. The crowd was now cheering and chanting and willing the team on to produce another goal to tie the aggregate score. A McIlroy goal was chalked off, and Frank Beattie had a sensational left-foot shot from thirty yards brilliantly turned over the bar by the 'keeper as the game developed into one-way traffic, but still an aggregate equaliser would not come. For a spell midway through the second half the pace dropped, and it looked as if their efforts had drained the Kilmarnock players' energy, but it was only a breather as they prepared to launch a *blitzkrieg* in the last fifteen minutes. With eighty minutes on the clock, McFadzean, only a stand-in for the injured Matt Watson, but playing magnificently (perhaps it was because Jim could perform so well in so many positions that he did not have a regular place in the side), pushed forward and played the ball to McIlroy wide out on the left wing. Brien slung over a superb cross to the far post and the incoming Jackie McInally met it with his head, giving the 'keeper no chance as Loy threw himself to his left in a vain attempt to block the powerful header. The aggregate score was now 4-4 and many of the younger members of the ecstatic crowd invaded the field and had to be pushed back off by the police. Kilmarnock were not finished and went in search of another goal. Young Tommy McLean smacked a right-foot shot off of Loy's left-hand post from a tight angle as the goalkeeper scrambled across goal. It was remarkable to witness the spectacle as only goalkeeper Forsyth and centre half McGrory remained aloof, and the nine other Killie players pinned the whole Eintracht team back within thirty yards of their goal for lengthy spells. At this time the 'away goals' rule did not exist, nor were penalty kicks used, so had the aggregate remained at 4-4 a third and deciding match would have been required. But Killie were not satisfied with that, and with just three minutes to go Schamer, helping out in defence, pulled down Sneddon on the edge of the box. Davie was hoping for a penalty kick but the referee gave only a free-kick on the edge of the area, and after he had picked himself up and regained his composure, he stabbed a short free-kick to Hamilton, and Ronnie's left-foot shot was deflected off the wall past Loy to make the score on the night 5-1, and another pitch invasion ensued. A few minutes later when the final whistle sounded on an astonishing 5-4 aggregate victory, the third pitch invasion of the night took place, as the police were unable to hold back the excited fans. This match was only seventeen-year-old Tommy McLean's third in the first team; his only previous appearances had come against Hibernian in the two legs of the Summer Cup semi-final in May, when he was sixteen. On a night when Killie had a team of stars, he perhaps shone brightest of all – with his phenomenal ball-skills he was a constant thorn in the side of the Germans, and over the next seven years he was an absolutely fundamental part of the team, until his inevitable transfer to

---

Kilmarnock: Forsyth, King, McFadzean, Murray, McGrory, Beattie, McLean, McInally, Hamilton, Sneddon, McIlroy.

Eintracht Frankfurt: Loy, Blusch, Herbert, Lindtner, Weber, Stinka, Kraus, Trimhold, Stein, Huberts, Schamer.

Souvenir Programme

•

FAIRS CITIES CUP
First Round—Second Leg

KILMARNOCK

versus

EINTRACHT

FRANKFURT

Rugby Park, Kilmarnock
Tuesday, 22nd September, 1964

KICK-OFF   ~   ~   7.30 p.m.

•

PROGRAMME   -   -   1/-

Programme for the match *v*. Eintracht.

Rangers. Eintracht had cracked completely under the weight of the constant pressure from a Kilmarnock team in which every player had contributed. The Germans played some attractive football, but by the end were disjointed. Their passing initially was good but apart from their goal the forwards had no other worthwhile shots. Only the fine performance of Loy saved Eintracht from an even heavier defeat. The visitors accepted their defeat sportingly and with good grace. It had been a quite remarkable triumph by Kilmarnock, and no other British side has ever come back from a four-goal deficit to progress to the next round of a European competition. In the next round Killie drew Everton, but could not recapture their Eintracht form and played rather poorly as a top-notch Everton side beat them home and away. But no football fan in Ayrshire over a certain age has ever forgotten 'THE EINTRACHT GAME'.

Killie's second goal against Eintracht scored by Brien McIlroy.

Killie's third goal was headed in by Jim McFadzean.

KILMARNOCK v. CELTIC

Date: 28 October 1964
Location: Rugby Park

Match title: Scottish League Division One

Celtic visited Rugby Park on Wednesday 28 October 1964 on League business. In recent seasons it had been anything but a happy hunting ground for the Parkhead club, who had lost 6-0 and 4-0 in their last two League visits. In addition, two League Cup fixtures in the same period had brought the Celts no joy either. Indeed, they had not even recorded a goal in any of the four games. Kilmarnock, on the other hand, had just announced that Willie Waddell had decided to retire from the manager's role at the end of the current season, and that the board had been reluctantly forced to accept his decision. It was a severe blow to Kilmarnock FC and it would be interesting to see what the effect would be on Waddell's players. At the time Killie were sitting at the top of the League with 7 wins and a draw from the first 8 matches, and were entertaining hopes of a first-ever League title after five years of near misses.

Referee W. Paterson of Bothwell set the game in motion under the Rugby Park floodlights with a crowd of 19,122 in attendance, and from early on it was clear that Waddell's decision to retire had, if anything, given the Killie players an extra incentive to win the Championship before he left. Their performance was akin to the Eintracht game of five weeks earlier, as Killie set about tormenting an unhappy Celtic defence. With only seven minutes played the home team took the lead. Ronnie Hamilton raced up the wing and laid the ball on to big Jackie McInally, who sent a great shot past the advancing John Fallon. On twenty-six minutes that lead became two when Jim Kennedy fouled McIlroy and Andy King's free-kick shot was deflected by Hamilton's head into the net. The Kilmarnock players, particularly McInally, Hamilton and McFadzean up front, were showing devastating form in a brilliant first-half display of precision football. With thirty-nine minutes played the score rose to 3-0 as a Sneddon corner kick caused confusion in the defence. The confusion ended when McIlroy headed the ball down to McInally, who sidestepped a defender beautifully and smashed a rocket-shot into the roof of the net. In the second half the one-sided nature of the game continued, and in fifty-three minutes Jim McFadzean, the man who could play almost anywhere, headed a fourth goal from a Davie Sneddon free-kick. Two minutes later Jim did it again – this time he headed in from a Sneddon corner and the score was 5-0 with thirty-five minutes to play. The game had been won and Killie now began to relax a little. Celtic had not been getting anywhere near Campbell Forsyth in the Kilmarnock goal and had to resort to long-range shots, one of which produced a goal for them from Tommy Gemmell, a man who, over the next few years, would net a large number of similar efforts for his team. With just over ten minutes remaining Charlie Gallagher netted a second for Celtic, also from long range, to give the score a slightly better look from the visiting perspective. Killie then pulled down the iron curtain and finished on top, the well-deserved winners 5-2, even if they were slightly annoyed by their laxness in the later stages. The win kept Killie at the top of the League after 9 matches. As for Celtic, who had actually lost the League Cup final 2-1 to Rangers on the previous Saturday, it was only the second defeat in their 9 matches.

Kilmarnock 5
McInally (2)
McFadzean (2)
Hamilton

Celtic 2
Gemmell
Gallagher

Left: Jackie McGrory, another stalwart. He was capped by Scotland three times and made 336 League appearances for Kilmarnock. *Right:* Andy King, a powerful full-back with Killie from 1960 to 1972. His League appearances total came to 221+1 as sub.

Kilmarnock had been particularly brilliant in the first half, and in the second half McFadzean's thrilling solo bursts through the middle had brought chaos to the Celtic defence. Hamilton at centre forward had given John Cushley the runaround, and Jackie McGrory had blotted out Stevie Chalmers. Matt Watson mastered the normally very tricky Jimmy Johnstone, and only Gallagher looked like he could hurt the home defence. Nevertheless it had been a highly entertaining game with seven goals that had thrilled the majority of the fans present. Early the following year, Jock Stein became Celtic manager, and the balance of power between these two clubs shifted dramatically – in fact it could almost be called a landslide, but Killie had enjoyed a few seasons of very marked supremacy over Celtic in meetings at Rugby Park. Within less than three years, six of the Celtic team from this match were the proud owners of European Cup-winner's medals, including Lisbon substitute John Fallon. Willie Waddell stuck to his decision to leave football management at the end of the season and became a football journalist, presumably a less stressful existence. Waddell returned to management in 1969 when his old club Rangers persuaded him to come back. However, for the rest of the 1964/65 season his players chased the League Championship in Willie's last year with Kilmarnock, and to discover how they fared see the next 'Classic Match'.

Kilmarnock: Forsyth, King, Watson, Murray, McGrory, Beattie, McIlroy, McInally, Hamilton, McFadzean, Sneddon.
Celtic: Fallon, Young, Gemmell, J. Brogan, Cushley, Kennedy, Johnstone, Murdoch, Chalmers, Gallagher, Lennox.

Hearts v. Kilmarnock

Date: 24 April 1965
Location: Tynecastle Park, Edinburgh

Match title: Scottish League Division One

With four second-place finishes in the League in the last five seasons, the Kilmarnock players went into the 1964/65 season desperate to finish winners, especially as one or two of the stalwarts so vital to Killie were entering the later stages of their careers. When it was made known that their much-respected manager Willie Waddell would be retiring on 30 June, they had additional motivation to do it this time.

They certainly began well. From an early stage Kilmarnock and Hearts pulled away from the others and took turns at holding top position in the League. Killie won their first 6 League games and remained undefeated until the fifteenth game. An extremely poor run in January and February saw them fall from grace, and three other clubs, Dunfermline, Hibs and most ominously Rangers, found themselves all in with a chance of the Championship along with Killie and Hearts in what had now become a five-way fight for the title. With only 8 games to be played, the Rugby Park team had fallen behind and the bookmakers were now quoting them at 25-1 to win the Championship. However, just as they had suddenly lost form, so they rediscovered it and won 6 and drew 1 of the next 7, leaving them going into the last day of the season in second place, 2 points behind Hearts. None of the other three clubs could now be Champions. As fate would have it, Kilmarnock's last fixture was against the Edinburgh club, away from home. Killie had to win at Tynecastle to go level on points, and the goal average was such that they had to win by a two-goal margin – a 1-0 or 2-1 Killie win would leave Hearts as Champions, but a 2-0 or 3-1 win (or better) would make Kilmarnock Champions for the first time ever. It was a tall order.

Although Hearts had scored more goals than Killie over the season and they were playing at home, the Ayrshire side were very confident going into the decider. After all, the sides had already met three times this season, twice in the League Cup and once in the League, and Killie had come out with two wins and a draw. They also had a fantastic team spirit, much of it due to the fact that over the last few seasons the composition of the team had not changed a great deal, and the players knew the strengths and weaknesses of each other intimately. Six of the players in the eleven were Ayrshire-born: Ferguson, King, Murray, McInally, Black and Sneddon, and another two who had made frequent appearances during the season but did not play at Tynecastle, Jim McFadzean and Ronnie Hamilton, were also born in the county. Interestingly, the last time the Championship had been decided on goal average had been in 1953 when Rangers had pipped Hibs by getting a late equaliser against Queen of the South to draw 1-1 and win on goal average. The scorer of Rangers' goal had been their right-winger Willie Waddell!

Although Hearts pushed forward at the start of the match their forwards seemed nervous, and dallied when in decent positions around the edge of the box. They had a near miss when Norwegian forward Jensen was put through on the right by Wallace, and despite the close attentions of McGrory and Watson he hit a flashing angled shot off Ferguson's left-hand post. At this point Hearts were giving it all they had and young Killie 'keeper Bobby Ferguson was showing why Campbell Forsyth,

Hearts 0	Kilmarnock 2
	Sneddon
	McIlroy

Programme for Hearts v. Kilmarnock, 1965.

Hearts: Cruickshank, Ferguson, Holt, Polland, Anderson, Higgins, Jensen, Barry, Wallace, Gordon, Hamilton.
Kilmarnock: Ferguson, King, Watson, Murray, McGrory, Beattie, McLean, McInally, Black, Sneddon, McIlroy.

who had played for Scotland earlier in the season, was being kept out of the side. Killie weathered Hearts' early pressure and began to look the more composed team, and while the home side may have had more goalscorers up front, they lacked the subtlety of the Kilmarnock forwards – Tommy McLean, Bertie Black and Davie Sneddon were full of craft and ingenuity. With twenty-seven minutes played Kilmarnock 'keeper Ferguson threw the ball out to McLean. Tommy made ground up the right and passed it inside to Brien McIlroy who in turn pushed it out to Jackie McInally, lurking wide on the right wing. McInally skipped past Polland and knocked the ball back in to McLean, who had made his way up into the box. McLean checked, looked up and floated a beautiful cross to the back post where Sneddon was on hand to head downwards past a helpless Jim Cruickshank. It was a rare Sneddon goal in that Davie seldom scored that way, preferring to keep the ball at his educated feet, but it was a very welcome departure from normality! Two minutes later Sneddon intercepted Roy Barry's short pass just inside Hearts' half of the field. He pushed the ball forward to Black, who evaded two Hearts players and squeezed a pass through to McIlroy, and Brien turned and hit a low left-foot shot into the far corner of the Hearts net. Hearts appealed rather half-heartedly for offside, but neither referee R.K. Wilson of Glasgow or anyone else gave any serious

Celebrations on the field after the final whistle. From left to right: Andy King, Bertie Black, Bobby Ferguson, Davie Sneddon (hugging manager Willie Waddell) and Hearts players Willie Wallace. The Killie player further in the background is Brien McIlroy.

thought to the claim. It may not have been the best goal McIlroy had ever scored for the club, but it was certainly the most valuable. With half an hour gone Killie had the two-goal lead required. On thirty-seven minutes the lead almost became three, but Cruickshank produced a magnificent diving save from a low Black shot and Killie remained 2-0 up at half-time.

The second half actually produced fewer goalmouth incidents than the first until near the end. Hearts played quite well, but spoiled it by hesitating or over-elaborating when near goal, and the accurate tackling and intelligent defending of King, Watson, McGrory and Beattie fairly easily contained the Hearts attack. Cruickshank produced another fine save from a point-blank McLean shot, but Tommy should really have given him no chance and scored. The quality of the football fell away a little, but both teams still showed superb fitness and loads of effort throughout. Hearts eventually began to crumble and so did their morale, and for the first time in the game some rough play, by Polland and Barry in particular, was witnessed. Roy Barry, a really lion-hearted player but now carrying an injury, had been lectured by the referee in the first half and was now 'sailing near the wind'. Anderson also got a ticking-off for holding Black by his jersey when he was going through – today it would be called a 'professional foul'. Time was moving remorselessly on; Kilmarnock still had their lead and the home side desperately needed a goal. Ferguson and McGrory of Kilmarnock were spoken to about time-wasting. The regulation ninety minutes were gone and the play entered injury-time. By now Killie had no interest in scoring themselves, it was just a matter of holding on for the final whistle, as one goal against them would swing the goal average back in Hearts' favour. McInally and McLean went down with cramp, 38,000 fans were gripped by tension and still play went on, until, with ninety-three minutes played, came one of the most dramatic moments in Scottish football history. Danny Ferguson launched a high ball into the Killie box, Frank Beattie jumped to head it away, but it skidded off his head straight to Hearts striker Alan Gordon, who hit a left-foot shot from only eight yards out. How many Ayrshire hearts stopped beating at this point will never be known, but somehow Bobby Ferguson threw himself across goal and pushed Gordon's shot round the post to safety. Film of the game shows defenders King, Watson and McGrory all simultaneously jumping into the air and throwing their arms out in a spontaneous reflex action as if trying to stop the shot themselves, even though they were yards away from the ball. It is remarkable footage of an even more remarkable save by a fantastic young goalkeeper. It must have been the most heart-stopping moment in the club's history and it signalled the end of Hearts' Championship hopes. Within seconds the final whistle had sounded after almost four minutes of time added on. Kilmarnock were 1964/65 League Champions, and the usually reserved Willie Waddell was racing on to the pitch to leap, jump and hug along with his ecstatic players. They were Champions by the margin of 0.042 of a goal, but it had been a deserved victory by the better-organised team. Hearts' players and officials showed terrific sportsmanship at the final whistle and also later in the dressing rooms, even though they must have been bitterly disappointed by the outcome. Hearts' best players had been Cruickshank, Anderson and Wallace. Kilmarnock's outstanding player was perhaps Frank Beattie, but they had all played well on Killie's most memorable day ever.

KILMARNOCK v. REAL MADRID

Date: 17 November 1965
Location: Rugby Park

Match title: European Cup First Round, First Leg

Winning the Scottish League Championship meant that Kilmarnock, under 'new' manager Malcolm MacDonald, who had returned from Brentford for his second spell in charge after the retirement of Willie Waddell, would now participate in the European Cup in season 1965/66. Their 'reward' was a trip to Albania to meet the local champions Nandori Tirana. If nothing else it proved to be a most interesting experience in a strange, mysterious land where conditions were not quite what Western Europeans were accustomed to. Having survived the trip to deepest Albania unscathed, Bertie Black ensured that Kilmarnock progressed through this preliminary round-tie in the second leg at Rugby Park. Killie awaited news of their first-round opponents, and were overjoyed when it went from the (slightly) ridiculous to the sublime, as the draw produced the magical name of Real Madrid, the then five-time winners of the cup.

The first leg against Real took place at Rugby Park, and unfortunately for the home side, they were forced to play it at a time when the twin pillars in the defence, Jackie McGrory and Frank Beattie, were both unavailable. This was a huge loss, as for several seasons they had been the strongest and most important part of the team, with captain Beattie in particular setting an example and proving an inspiration to all his colleagues. Beattie was unable to shrug off a niggling injury and McGrory had not re-signed for the club at the start of the season in time to be eligible to play in the European matches.

Kilmarnock started off the match by throwing everything at the Spanish Champions. With eight minutes on the clock Ronnie Hamilton lofted the ball over to Brien McIlroy, who instantly fired a superb strike into the corner of the net. To the utter dismay and disbelief of most of the 24,325 crowd, the West German linesman decided that McIlroy was in an offside position. The crowd let their feelings be known with howls of abuse directed at the officials. In what could probably be described as a surprise development, it was the normally flamboyant, attacking Spanish side who were being forced backwards to the extent that for most of the first half they had seven players in defence and were hitting back only in occasional breakaways. Eighteen-year-old Tommy McLean on Killie's right-wing was at his brilliant best; so good in fact that the Madrid defenders eventually had to resort to robust tactics in an attempt to subdue him, but even that did not succeed in stopping Tommy from tormenting the Real defence throughout the game. Jackie McInally and Ronnie Hamilton also gave the visitors a hard time, and their Argentinian-born centre half, the huge and highly rated Jose Santamaria, could do little with Kilmarnock-born Hamilton all through the game. It was Killie's night, and they dominated as shots flew in from all angles. Real's only attacking contribution in the first twenty minutes ended with a snap shot from Francisco Gento which caught everyone by surprise except goalkeeper Bobby Ferguson, who saved well. Driven on by outstanding midfielders O'Connor and McFadzean, it seemed that a goal had to come and it duly arrived from the penalty spot, when McInally was dragged down in the penalty area by Sanchiz and McLean coolly stroked the ball along the ground

Kilmarnock 2
McLean (pen)
McInally

Real Madrid 2
Martinez
Amancio

Jackie McInally heads the ball past Betancourt of Real Madrid to make the score 2-2. The other Killie player in the picture is Brien McIlroy.

just inside the left-hand corner of Antonio Betancourt's goal. It was no more than the home side deserved for their almost total dominance up to this point. Perhaps it was just the wake-up call that the Spaniards required, as within four minutes a team that had never been in the game suddenly produced an equaliser. A neat spell of short combination passes through the middle involving Ferenc Puskas and Ruiz led to an opening being created for Jose Martinez (also known as 'Pirri') to evade Matt Watson and crack a right-foot shot high past Ferguson. Nevertheless, Kilmarnock remained in command and numerous shots were fired at the Real goal. However Killie's luck was out, and they had to go in at half-time somewhat disappointed, given the run of play, with a score of 1-1.

With fifty-three minutes gone Ignacio Zoco blatantly floored McInally, who looked set to score, inside the penalty area, but it seemed that German referee G. Schulenburg believed that one penalty kick per game was enough for any team and he ignored the very strong appeals, despite the fact that it was a much clearer offence than the one for which he had already awarded a penalty kick.

Kilmarnock: Ferguson, King, Watson, O'Connor, Murray, McFadzean, McLean, McInally, Hamilton, Sneddon, McIlroy.
Real Madrid: Betancourt, Miera, Sanchiz, Ruiz, Santamaria, Zoco, Amancio, Martinez, Grosso, Puskas, Gento.

Almost immediately after, on fifty-five minutes, came a shock for Kilmarnock when Real broke away again and the ball was played out into a large space on the left wing for the flying winger Gento to run onto so speedily that he looked as if he must be on a bicycle. Gento crossed the ball in towards the near post where Amancio and Murray both went for it, only for the ball to fly into the net past a helpless Ferguson. Amancio naturally claimed the goal, although the suspicion that it had also come off Murray could not be avoided, and despite all that had gone before Madrid were now ahead. It should be said that Eric Murray, playing at centre half for the first time and standing-in as captain in the absence of McGrory and Beattie, was an inspiration to his fellow defenders when confronted by the very rare, but admittedly very highly skilled Real forward play, and no blame could be attached to him for this goal. The Real lead did not last long. On sixty minutes Hamilton swivelled and turned to create space for himself at the corner of the Madrid penalty area, and hit a high cross from the right towards the far post. Betancourt was caught in two minds – he thought of coming to get it, but hesitated, and big Jackie McInally came in to head the ball downwards past the 'keeper. The Killie support went wild at this deserved equaliser, and they roared their team on in an attempt to obtain the first-leg lead they merited. On seventy-three minutes Gento was booked for a rash tackle on Tommy McLean, the man Real just could not pin down, as the Spaniards fought to hang on for a draw. Despite all Killie's efforts another goal would not come and the game finished in a 2-2 draw, not on the face of it a bad result for Kilmarnock, but nevertheless a let-down considering the way the play had gone. Ruiz and Amancio had been the visitors' best men on the night, and the game had been a thriller and fairly warmed-up the crowd on a cold evening, but was ultimately disappointing for Kilmarnock who had hoped to win this match and thus complete the double of European victories over both the sides involved in that legendary European Cup final at Hampden in 1960, having of course already beaten the Germans, Eintracht. This was a match Kilmarnock really should have won.

As was widely anticipated, Real won the second leg in the vast Bernabeau Stadium in Madrid. Killie started off really well and took the lead through Brien McIlroy, who later won a penalty kick which Tommy McLean then missed. Errors in defence, where McGrory and Beattie were still unavailable, and by

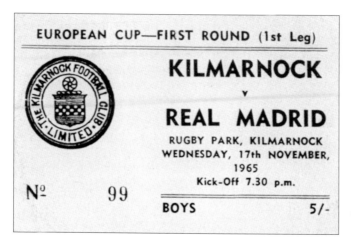

Ticket for Kilmarnock v. Real Madrid.

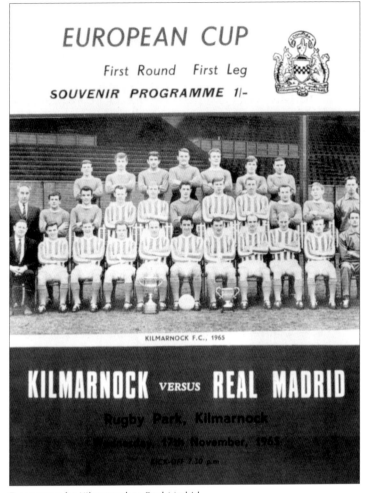

Programme for Kilmarnock v. Real Madrid.

Bobby Ferguson, who had by his own high standards a poor game, saw them eventually lose 5-1 (agg. 7-3). The legendary Hungarian Ferenc Puskas did not play in the second leg in Spain – the match at Rugby Park turned out to be his last-ever European tie. Real Madrid went on to win the European Cup, beating Partizan Belgrade 2-1 in the final in Brussels. It was the sixth time they had lifted the trophy.

KILMARNOCK v. ROYAL ANTWERP

Date: 2 November 1966
Location: Rugby Park

Match title: Fairs Cities Cup Second Round,
Second Leg

Kilmarnock had won the first leg of this Fairs Cities Cup tie in Belgium 1-0 on Tuesday 25 October 1966 with a goal scored by Jackie McInally. Naturally, having been victorious away from home, Killie were firm favourites to qualify for the next round. The first leg, however, had been a bad-tempered, niggly affair with several unsavoury incidents between the players, particularly between goalscorer McInally and Goris of Antwerp, the man nominated as his marker.

With only one minute gone in the second leg Killie's Craig Watson hit the post with a fine header after McLean had romped down the right wing and crossed the ball to him beautifully. Was this the shape of things to come? The answer seemed to be yes, as with only six minutes played McInally raced onto a through ball from Gerry Queen, strode past the defence and hit a superb low shot into the net from almost twenty-five yards. Then, on seventeen minutes, Renier foolishly brought down left-winger Watson in the box and Queen converted the resulting penalty kick. Killie's place in the next round already seemed assured. Antwerp then had a bright spell around the half-hour mark without actually scoring, but it was only a prelude to Kilmarnock putting the game even further out of their reach when, with thirty-two minutes played, Killie burst into attack and Tommy McLean gathered a magnificent pass from McInally and streaked through to hammer an unstoppable shot from around sixteen yards past Cooremans. The underlying tensions between the teams surfaced in forty minutes when Queen was booked for a foul on Segers, who was forced to limp off. He returned later, but before the end of the match he limped off once more. When the whistle sounded for half-time Kilmarnock led 3-0 on the night and 4-0 on aggregate.

The second half commenced with an amazing run by McLean, a player Antwerp simply could not cope with. He sliced open the visitors' defence, but his colleagues did not take advantage of his fine cross and the chance of another goal was gone. McLean really was a phenomenal football talent; capable of the most astonishing feats of ball-control, and his accuracy from 'dead-ball' situations would have had even David Beckham envious. It was shameful that Tommy only received six full international caps for Scotland, even if he had as rivals for the right-winger spot Jimmy Johnstone of Celtic and Willie Henderson of Rangers.

On forty-eight minutes a visiting defender deliberately handled the ball inside the box when there appeared to be no immediate danger. McLean converted the penalty kick with ease. Just one minute later McInally got his second goal when he beat the goalkeeper to a long through-pass from Killie's Danish forward Carl Bertelsen and struck it into the net. Two more minutes and the score rose to 6-0 – this was the third goal inside just six minutes of the start of the second half! This time Queen scored after more magnificent set-up play by the wizard McLean. With Kilmarnock so obviously superior to their Belgian opponents and clearly set for the next round, one would have thought that the match would peter out, but that was not the case, as on sixty-seven minutes an explosive incident occurred. McInally and Goris clashed at the byline with the ball out of play – it was almost certainly a sequel to the problems between the same two men in the first leg in Belgium.

Kilmarnock 7
McInally (2), Queen (2, 1 pen)
McLean (2, 1 pen), C. Watson

Royal Antwerp 2
Beyers
Van De Velde

Jackie McInally, who entertained the crowds at Rugby Park from 1959 to 1967, but unfortunately got himself sent off against Royal Antwerp when he could no longer tolerate being spat on and kicked.

Whatever actually took place, and it was not clear to the vast majority of those present, Jackie McInally was ordered to leave the field by referee R. Machin of France. The problem was Jackie did not want to go! Feeling himself to be the victim of an injustice, he at first refused to leave the field, and it was only after captain Frank Beattie and then trainer Walter McCrae spoke with him at some length that he slowly trudged off. It was particularly unfortunate that Jackie, who had scored twice in this match as well as scoring the only goal of the first leg, had been sent off, as he had terrorised the Antwerp defence all evening. He and Tommy McLean had been the best players on the field. Perhaps the referee had been right to take stern action, for the game had been threatening to get out of control, but it looked as if there had been faults on both sides with severe provocation involved.

In the sixty-ninth minute Craig Watson brought Kilmarnock's tally up to seven when a high lob from near the touchline deceived the goalkeeper and dropped into the net. It may well have been intended as a cross for a team-mate; nevertheless it made the score 7-0 on the night and 8-0 on aggregate. Surprisingly the Belgians hit back, and on seventy-three minutes they reduced the deficit when Beyers beat Ferguson from close range as the Killie defence was caught napping, and then on seventy-eight minutes they further reduced the margin of defeat with a goal from Van De Velde. However, Kilmarnock went through to the third round on a very healthy 8-2 aggregate, and 11,963 fans had enjoyed a thoroughly exciting match packed full of incident.

Kilmarnock: Ferguson, King, McFadzean, O'Connor, McGrory, Beattie, McLean, McInally, Bertelsen, Queen, C. Watson.

Royal Antwerp: Cooremans, Renier, Bohez, Geens, Renes, Goris, Beyers, Van Moer, Frankel, Segers, Van De Velde.

Kilmarnock v. Rangers

Date: 11 February 1967   **Match title:** Scottish League Division One
Location: Rugby Park

The Prime Minister of the Soviet Union, Alexei Kosygin, visited Britain in February 1967 on a mission aimed at improving relations between the two countries, as they had been somewhat less than totally cordial since the end of the Second World War and the imposition of the so-called 'Cold War'. Included in sixty-two-year-old Mr Kosygin's schedule was a visit to Scotland, and he had expressed an interest in attending a football match while there, as he had apparently always been a keen football enthusiast. Thus it was that his itinerary was arranged to allow this, and it was decided that the Kilmarnock v. Rangers match at Rugby Park was the most suitable occasion, and the arrangements were made. It was no straightforward task for the home club – as can be imagined, security concerns were paramount and a large number of season-ticket holders were unable to use their normal seats. The rigorous security required dictated that the Prime Minister had to be well surrounded by bodyguards, and legend has it that many large men sat throughout the match with one-hand inside their coats, ready should they be called upon to protect their boss. On the whole, the people who had to give up their normal seats for this special occasion understood the situation and the importance of the visit, and the day went well. Mr Kosygin went onto the field to be introduced to the players and officials, including referee R.H. Davidson of Airdrie, before the match, albeit surrounded by his large entourage, and he then returned to his seat to enjoy a cracking match played in front of 31,551 fans.

In the early stages it was Rangers who looked brightest, but they found Killie goalkeeper Bobby Ferguson to be in magnificent form. Ferguson twisted in mid-air and used his fingertips to push a Dave Smith rocket round the post, and then he dived and held young Sandy Jardine's fierce shot soon after. Seconds later he was called on to grab the ball off the toes of Alex Willoughby, and then had to brilliantly save a twenty-five-yard shot from Rangers skipper John Greig. Ferguson was looking every inch the international goalkeeper he was, and he was still only twenty-two years old. In reply to Rangers' numerous goal attempts, all Killie had to show was a Brien McIlroy header and a shot from ex-Rangers player Craig Watson, both of which went over the bar, although with McIlroy's it was only very narrowly over. Norrie Martin, in goal for Rangers, had in contrast a comparatively easy time. Before the interval Ferguson produced further fine saves from another Greig shot and yet another dive to fingertip away a Willoughby first-time effort. It began to look as if he could not be beaten and the teams went in at half-time locked at 0-0.

Kilmarnock now had the wind at their backs, but Rangers were desperate to take both points from this game to reduce the 3-point gap between themselves and Celtic at the top of the League table. Ten minutes into the second half the breakthrough came for them when, from a fine side-footed Jardine pass, Willie Henderson broke away on the right and sent over a high lob towards the top right-hand corner of Ferguson's goal. The 'keeper did really well to get a hand to the ball and push it out, but international winger Davie Wilson was on the spot to lash the ball back high into the net. The visitors' tails were up and Willoughby almost made it 2-0 straight after when he hit the junction of bar and upright with a rasping shot.

Kilmarnock 1	Rangers 2
McIlroy	*Wilson*
	Willoughby

Rangers' Alex Smith and Killie's Gerry Queen in action. Note how the crowd has spilled onto the edge of the pitch.

Kilmarnock: Ferguson, King, McFadzean, Murray, McGrory, Beattie, McLean, McInally, Queen, C. Watson, McIlroy. Sub not used: Dickson.
Rangers: Martin, Johansen, Provan, Jardine, McKinnon, Greig, Henderson, Willoughby, A. Smith, D. Smith, Wilson. Sub not used: Unknown.

KILMARNOCK v. RANGERS

Having absorbed so much pressure, Killie at last began to fight back determinedly and Eric Murray hit a tremendous shot that was net-bound until Ronnie McKinnon popped up on the line to head clear. Then, with seventy-one minutes played, Tommy McLean sent over a wicked hanging corner from the left. Up went a cluster of players from both teams, and it seemed that it was Killie's Gerry Queen who got his head to it to touch it on towards McIlroy, who sneaked in to smartly head an equaliser. McIlroy had a chance to score again minutes later but his shot flew into the side-netting. The home side were now enjoying their best spell of the match, throwing caution to the wind, and the action really heated up with Rangers temporarily on the ropes. Perversely it was Rangers who got the next goal on seventy-seven minutes. It was a scrambled affair – McKinnon lobbed a free-kick into the box from around halfway and it dropped tantalisingly near the six-yard line, Ferguson and Jackie McGrory seemed unsure which of them was dealing with it and Willoughby took advantage of their indecision as the ball bounced to get involved, and he claimed a goal with the faintest of touches with his head, helping the ball to trickle over the line. Willoughby had now scored 7 goals in his last 3 games, and he was certainly the current pin-up boy of the Ibrox fans. It was a bad break for the home side and the goal was followed by a pitch invasion by hundreds of jubilant Rangers fans, just as had happened after their first goal. On that occasion Davie Wilson had been slightly injured by his own fans and Rangers coach Bobby Seith had been required to run onto the pitch to try to protect his players. The

Mr Kosygin shakes hands with Jackie McGrory. Other players are, from left to right: Beattie, Ferguson, King, McFadzean (partly hidden by McGrory) and McInally.

winning goal was not really worthy of deciding such a titanic struggle, but the points went to Rangers 2-1. While defensively the two teams were well-matched, Rangers' forwards were much more dangerous than Killie's. The pitch was heavily sanded and had been all against a smooth, passing type of game; nevertheless the teams had managed to produce a thriller that was a credit to them both. Rangers had deserved the victory, but it had never been easy, especially with Bobby Ferguson in such great form. He had been totally outstanding, apart from his unfortunate misjudgement at the winning goal. Killie's other top performers were Andy King, Jim McFadzean and Tommy McLean. The positional switch of Alex Smith and Alex Willoughby had been decisive in Rangers' win – when the latter had moved up front and Smith dropped back to midfield they had functioned much better. At the end of the season Ferguson was transferred to West Ham United for a £65,000 fee, which was said at the time to be a world-record fee for a goalkeeper. Strangely, Bobby did not perhaps do as well in London as his many admirers expected. He got off to a poor start, admittedly playing in front of a notoriously suspect defence, even with the great Bobby Moore in it, and never showed quite the same form as he had displayed in Scotland, although he remained with the Hammers for around fourteen years, during which time he spent long spells out of the first team. Tellingly, he never gained another international cap after leaving Kilmarnock, although he had looked as if he would be Scotland's goalkeeper for years to come when he left Killie.

For all their hard-won 2 points from this game, Rangers remained 3 points behind Celtic, who went on to retain the Championship at the end of the season in addition to winning the League Cup, Scottish Cup and, of course, the European Cup. Celtic, incidentally, had beaten Ayr United 5-0 at Somerset Park on the same afternoon as the Killie v. Rangers match. It must have been quite a day for the Ayrshire police!

As for Mr Kosygin, he was quoted after the match as saying 'It was a very hard game. I thoroughly enjoyed it'. He had seemed especially pleased when, during the game, the fans chanted rhythmically 'Kos-y-gin, Kos-y-gin, Kos-y-gin'. He beamed and shook his hands above his head in a boxer's salute. Not only had the Soviet Prime Minister been there, we also had a King and Queen present – check out the Kilmarnock line-up! It had been a great occasion.

Leeds United v. Kilmarnock

Date: 19 May 1967   **Match title:** Fairs Cities Cup Semi-Final, First Leg
Location: Elland Road, Leeds

After disposing of two Belgian clubs, Royal Antwerp and La Gantoise, and then the East Germans Locomotiv Leipzig, Kilmarnock drew Leeds United in the semi-final of the Fairs Cities Cup. The club was delighted to have drawn such highly rated opponents; it was sure to be a money-spinner and in addition did not involve them in any great travel difficulties. Killie were fully aware of how difficult a task they faced, as the last few seasons had seen Leeds continually challenging for major honours in England, and they had been in the semi-final of this same competition one year before. Their line-up was packed with well-known names, internationals such as Gary Sprake, Paul Madeley, Billy Bremner, Jackie Charlton, Norman Hunter, Peter Lorimer, Johnny Giles and Eddie Gray.

The first leg was played at Elland Road on a Friday evening. Continuous heavy rain meant that the game was never going to be one for the connoisseurs as the pitch turned into a sea of mud, but while it would not provide classy, flowing football, it was a rip-roaring he-man battle, and the crowd loved almost every minute. Both teams had reputations for tight defences, but on this occasion the reputations seemed ill-founded as both committed a number of uncharacteristic errors, only partially due to the poor ground conditions. No less than four Kilmarnock forwards had been receiving treatment for injuries in the week leading up to the game. In the event, Gerry Queen and Brien McIlroy made it, but Tommy McLean and Jackie McInally missed the match. The loss of McLean was a particularly bad blow as he was the mastermind behind all Killie's attacking plans. Craig Watson and Pat O'Connor, normally a half-back, came in to form a new right wing. For Leeds, World Cup-winning centre half Jackie Charlton and striker Jimmy Greenhoff were injured, and they were replaced by the extraordinarily versatile Madeley, who was almost always in the team somewhere anyway, and by Yorkshire-born Rod Belfitt.

43,189 were present as referee J.F. Dorpmans of Holland started the match, and within one minute he was blowing for the first goal after the powerful Belfitt got above goalkeeper Bobby Ferguson and Jackie McGrory to head Johnny Giles' cross into the net. A very poor start for the visitors was soon made even worse with four minutes played when the same player got his second goal. This time he dived low to head in a Mike O'Grady cross. The shocked Kilmarnock defenders looked at each other in horror and wondered what exactly was going on. Eventually they settled and set about working their way back into the game, and were rewarded in twenty-one minutes when McIlroy, who loved to wander all over the front line and was not strictly speaking a winger, showed his goal-grabbing ability, popping up in front of goal to slip home a fine Carl Bertelsen cross. McIlroy and Bertelsen almost scored again with separate opportunities but it was United who struck next on thirty-one minutes when a disastrous Killie blunder allowed Belfitt to complete his hat-trick. Then Leeds returned the compliment on thirty-six minutes when a foolish Gray pass-back to Sprake stuck in the mud and the ever-alert McIlroy got to it first, rounded Willie Bell and gave Sprake no chance with a powerful shot. The score was now 3-2, but within two more minutes it was 4-2 when international centre half McGrory needlessly handled a high cross and Giles made no mistake from the spot. Six goals in only thirty-

---

Leeds United 4
Belfitt (3)
Giles (pen)

Kilmarnock 2
McIlroy (2)

eight minutes – how many more goals could this semi-final produce? In the event the answer was none! Once the two managers got their players into the dressing rooms at half-time one can only imagine what was said to certain normally very reliable defenders. As conditions worsened the match got tougher and tougher. Billy Bremner downed Pat O'Connor, but in O'Connor he was meeting exactly the same type of player as himself and the hard, fearless O'Connor later got his own back on his fellow Scot. Both defences were more like their normal selves in the second half and chances were scarcer; however, with two minutes to go Killie's Queen hit a post, and in the dying seconds O'Grady hit the bar. Bremner, now operating at centre forward, also struck a post to end this thriller. The players left the field with the crowd standing and cheering twenty-two mud-splattered gladiators off, and it was a deserved ovation as it had been great entertainment. The two managers made almost identical comments to the press after the game, to the effect that 'We'll never give away goals like that again'.

The second leg at Kilmarnock was another tough, physical but nevertheless engrossing struggle that again had the crowd roaring. Kilmarnock naturally did most of the attacking, but Leeds, who had brought in Terry Cooper in O'Grady's place to act as an extra defender, denied them the two goals they needed. The game finished 0-0 and Leeds went through to face Dynamo Zagreb in the final, which did not take place until the following season.

Programme for Leeds v. Kilmarnock.

Leeds United: Sprake, Reaney, Bell, Bremner, Madeley, Hunter, O'Grady, Lorimer, Belfitt, Giles, Gray.

Kilmarnock: Ferguson, King, McFadzean, Murray, McGrory, Beattie, C. Watson, O'Connor, Bertelsen, Queen, McIlroy.

RANGERS v. KILMARNOCK

Date: 21 September 1968
Location: Ibrox Park

Match title: Scottish League Division One

Both sides were playing their third League game of the season, after experiencing mixed fortunes in the early season League Cup matches. Rangers, though, must have gone into the game on a high, having beaten Celtic and then the Yugoslavs Vojvodina within the past week. Naturally the home side were expected to win the game, especially as Killie's form so far had been very up and down. Early on it looked as if the visitors were going to give one of their better performances as Jim McLean struck a low shot narrowly wide after John Gilmour and little Jimmy Cook had performed a slick one-two movement, and Killie continued to show sweet-moving play which must have impressed those present. Rangers, on the other hand, seemed to rely too much on power-play, and it failed to achieve anything throughout the first half of the game, during which the only thing they had to show for all their effort was a Willie Henderson header, brilliantly held just under the bar by Sandy McLaughlan. On the half-hour mark the visitors deservedly went ahead. Roger Hynd, harassed by Gerry Queen, tried to play a square pass to Ronnie McKinnon twenty yards away, but he made a bit of a mess of it, sending the ball to Killie's Eddie Morrison instead. Eddie, who would actually have been offside had he received it from a colleague instead of an opponent, controlled it smartly, ran in on goal and knocked the ball past the helpless Norrie Martin of Rangers. Continuing to play a neat brand of controlled football, Kilmarnock held their 1-0 lead until half-time.

Rangers came out more determined at the start of the second half and Swede Orjan Persson's drive forced McLaughlan into making a fine diving save. Then, on fifty-nine minutes, Killie went two ahead and it was that man Morrison again. With a wonderful solo run from the halfway line he went down the right, and with the defence expecting a cross, he cut in and slipped the ball past Martin again. Two goals down, Rangers threw caution to the wind and launched themselves at the Kilmarnock goal, and got the break they were seeking with a fluke. Persson pushed a short pass to Willie Johnston, but with his path to goal blocked, Johnston had little option but to try a shot from twenty-five yards. He did not get hold of the shot properly and it appeared to offer no danger, but somehow McLaughlan, who had an otherwise excellent match, allowed the ball to slip between his legs. Sandy was left holding his head when he would have much preferred to be holding the ball! Rangers had just the lift they needed and the large majority of the 40,000 crowd got right behind them as they let themselves be heard. On seventy-three minutes, Sandy Jardine, who at the time was being tried at centre forward, made his only real contribution to the match when he was on the spot, a few yards from goal, to ram the ball high into the net after McLaughlan had parried an Andy Penman drive. Then, with just over ten minutes remaining, McLaughlan punched away an inswinging Persson corner straight to Henderson, and Willie returned a fifteen-yard shot low into the net. Despite playing classy football Killie now found they had gone from 2-0 up to 3-2 down inside a stunning fifteen-minute spell. Even though the game had cruelly swung away from Kilmarnock, they still had something left. Out on the right, Morrison picked up a pass from Gilmour and raced into the

Rangers 3	Kilmarnock 3
Johnston	*Morrison (2)*
Jardine	*Queen (pen)*
Henderson	

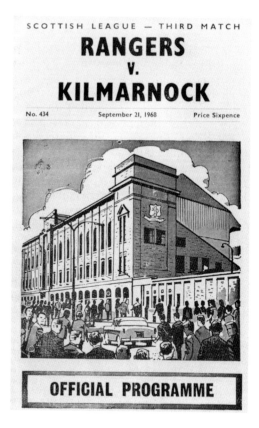

SCOTTISH LEAGUE — THIRD MATCH

RANGERS
v.
KILMARNOCK

No. 434   September 21, 1968   Price Sixpence

OFFICIAL PROGRAMME

Programme for the Rangers match.

penalty area, beating McKinnon, who had been unable to cope with the aggressive Killie striker throughout, and just as Morrison was picking his spot, the powerful Roger Hynd came across and upended him. It was a clear-cut affair and little protest was made as referee Thomson of Edinburgh awarded a penalty kick. With only five minutes left the pressure on Killie's Gerry Queen was immense as he stepped up to take the kick, and he made no mistake. Even though goalkeeper Martin managed to get a touch on the ball he could not prevent the well-placed shot from going in to make the score 3-3. The visitors then had to survive two very late scares when Rangers full-back Colin Jackson, up with the attack, got into good shooting positions twice in the last minute, but he blew his chance of glory both times. The one booking in a very clean match went to the normally reserved Andy Penman for a show of dissent. Kilmarnock had performed admirably, especially McLaughlan (apart from the first goal), King, Gilmour, McGrory, T. McLean, Morrison and the lion-hearted Cook. They must have left Ibrox with mixed feelings however, having played so well and been two goals up, but then being behind with only five minutes left and salvaging a draw. Was it a good result or a bad one?

Rangers: Martin, Jackson, Johansen, Greig, McKinnon, Hynd, Henderson, Penman, Jardine, Johnston, Persson. Sub not used: Willoughby.
Kilmarnock: McLaughlan, King, Dickson, Gilmour, McGrory, Arthur, T. McLean, Queen, Morrison, J. McLean, Cook. Sub not used: Rodman.

Kilmarnock v. Raith Rovers

Date: 26 October 1968   **Match title:** Scottish League Division One
Location: Rugby Park

Kilmarnock's inconsistent start to the 1968/69 season continued, one week brilliant, next week mediocre. The highs and lows were never better demonstrated than in the eighth League match of the season at home to Raith Rovers, when the team managed to show both sides of their game in the one match. Manager Walter McCrae, in his first full season in charge having taken over in March, must have been tearing his hair out. There was no question at all about the fact that they had some excellent players, particularly Dickson, McGrory, Beattie, Gilmour, Queen and the McLean brothers Jim and Tommy, and were capable of playing some magnificent football, such as in the recent 3-3 draw at Ibrox, but they were susceptible to defeat against lesser teams.

The inspirational Frank Beattie was left out of the starting eleven and was the one substitute allowed per team at that time. Young Robin Arthur retained possession of the number six shirt for another week. Quite what went wrong in the normally pretty secure Kilmarnock defence that day is hard to say. With no disrespect to Raith Rovers, a team that Killie were normally expected to beat at home, it must have come as a shock to fans throughout Scotland when the half-time scoreboards revealed the following astonishing scoreline: Kilmarnock 0 Raith Rovers 4. George Falconer had been the Rovers hero in that first half. He netted a goal in eight minutes following a David Millar pass, although there was some suspicion that he may have been offside on that one. On twenty-three minutes he scored again – Billy Dickson made a mess of a pass-back, Falconer pounced, and at the second attempt got the ball into the net off goalkeeper McLaughlan's legs. Between those two goals, Raith 'keeper Bobby Reid had made two wonderful saves from Tommy McLean and John Gilmour, and full-back Tom Hislop had cleared a McIlroy shot off the line. Nine minutes after his second goal Falconer completed his hat-trick with the best goal of the trio, when he latched on to a beautiful Gordon Wallace pass and struck a magnificent low left-foot shot from twenty yards into the net. Killie's attempt at a revival again stalled when McIlroy's shot hit the post, and then Hislop again cleared off the line, this time from Jim McLean. The ineptness of Kilmarnock's defending was further highlighted a minute before the interval when Jim Gillespie hit a left-foot shot through a crowd of players and the ball went in off a post. Killie left the field at the interval with the jeers of the fans ringing in their ears. Frank Beattie came on for the second half in place of Robin Arthur.

Rarely can a single substitution have made such a difference to a game. The hesitancy in the Kilmarnock defence was miraculously cured, and the Raith forwards who had dominated so much now found they could hardly get a touch of the ball. It took until the fifty-seventh minute for the difference to be reflected in the score, Cook was brought down in the box by Jackie Bolton and Tommy McLean, who had been Killie's most dangerous forward in the first half, but got little response from the other forwards, scored from the penalty kick. Beattie realised that getting the ball to McLean was the key to success and he spent the rest of the half doing exactly that whenever possible. On sixty-seven minutes the bold Eddie Morrison threw himself at Brien McIlroy's chip and headed in Killie's

---

Kilmarnock 4
McLean (2, 1 pen)
Morrison
McIlroy

       Raith Rovers 4
      Falconer (3)
      Gillespie

second goal. Rovers were now very nervous and began to indulge in time-wasting, and for a spell it seemed that although they were under great pressure Raith were going to hold out. However, with six minutes left to play Jimmy Cook shot hard across goal from the left and McIlroy was on hand a few yards out to force the ball over the line for his belated first goal of the season. The home fans were ecstatic, sensing that the game could yet be salvaged as Killie set up a furious assault on the Rovers goal. In the last minute Tommy McLean, who had again wandered out on to the left wing, took possession, transferred the ball to his right foot and from eighteen yards hit a shot through a wall of defenders into the net to send the crowd berserk. The team that left the field to jeers at half-time left to loud, prolonged cheers at full-time. How had such a transformation been possible? Perhaps a better question would be how had Kilmarnock managed to find themselves four goals down at the break? One thing that was not in question was that Tommy McLean had shown that he fully deserved his place in Scotland's World Cup pool of players for the upcoming qualifying matches.

Programme for Kilmarnock v. Raith Rovers, 1968.

Kilmarnock: McLaughlan, King, Dickson, Gilmour, McGrory, Arthur (Beattie), T. McLean, Cook, Morrison, J. McLean, McIlroy.
Raith Rovers: Reid, Hislop, Gray, Millar, Polland, Bolton, Wilson, Falconer, Wallace, Sneddon, Gillespie. Sub not used: Judge.

KILMARNOCK v. RANGERS

Date: 4 January 1969   **Match title:** Scottish League Division One
Location: Rugby Park

When Rangers visited Rugby Park early in1969 they were sitting in fourth place in the League and Kilmarnock were fifth. However, it was a very tight situation at the top of the table as leaders Celtic had only 5 points more than sixth-placed St Mirren. Killie and Rangers had fought out a thrilling 3-3 draw at Ibrox earlier in the season, a match that would be very hard to beat for thrills and excitement, but they managed it! It was to be described by the newspapers as 'the most exciting game of the season', and if anything, that was an understatement.

With only seven minutes played Rangers took the lead. Orjan Persson and Willie Henderson's interpassing moved them down the right wing. Persson passed inside to Willie Johnston, whose half-hit shot was blocked, only for it to break back out to Andy Penman, who smashed a low shot past the unsighted Killie 'keeper Sandy McLaughlan. Eight minutes later the home side equalised with a goal of breathtaking brilliance. Tommy McLean won a free-kick just outside the box, and taking it himself, he coolly chipped the ball over the defensive wall, curling it slightly out towards the left. Killie left-back Billy Dickson raced forward past the wall and got to the spinning ball a few yards from the byline and smashed a raging left-foot shot high into the Rangers net from a tight angle. This amazing goal had clearly been pre-planned by the two men, who had signed for the club at the same time, from the same club and travelled to training together every day. Clearly they discussed more than the weather on their journeys. A lot of heavy tackles were flying in from both sides, but a lot of great football and a high degree of artistic play was also on view in this cracker of a game. On twenty-seven minutes Rangers took the lead again. Dickson won a tackle against Henderson, but referee J. Callaghan of Glasgow ruled it a foul. Kai Johansen knocked the free-kick into the box, where Willie Johnston and Frank Beattie went for it with their heads. Johnston missed it but the ball unluckily hit off Beattie and rolled over the line. Rangers were now firing on all cylinders and enjoyed their best spell of the game – McLaughlan was forced to pull off a fantastic save from a Willie Mathieson rocket-shot. However, Kilmarnock managed to survive Rangers' onslaught unscathed, and equalised on forty-two minutes when McIlroy cut the ball inside to Eddie Morrison, and John Greig pulled him down for a clear-cut penalty kick. Tommy McLean made his customary competent job from the spot as goalkeeper Norrie Martin went the wrong way. The half-time respite was badly needed by players and fans from both clubs as they went in for a well-deserved breather tied at 2-2.

The second half proved to be just as fast and incident-packed as the first. In the early stages it was a confident-looking Killie who had the better of the play, and they should have gone ahead for the first time when McIlroy put Gerry Queen through with a wonderful opportunity to score, but Martin got to his shot to tip it past the post. Then Rangers took the lead again with sixty-one minutes on the clock. Johnston and Stein broke away and set-up Persson, who slammed a low shot past McLaughlan. Six minutes later Rangers sent on Sandy Jardine in place of the goalscorer. The question now was could Killie equalise for a third time? On seventy-three minutes we had our answer – from a McLean corner on the left

Kilmarnock 3	Rangers 3
Dickson	*Penman*
McLean (pen)	*Beattie (og)*
McIlroy	*Persson*

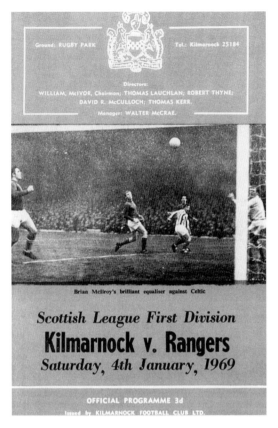

A particularly interesting programme cover for the match v. Rangers, showing Killie's equaliser in the recent 1-1 draw at Parkhead.

Queen got his head to the ball, but Greig headed it off the line only for the razor-sharp McIlroy to get to it first and knock it into the net to level the score at 3-3.

Four minutes later came the most controversial incident of the match. Colin Stein badly fouled Tommy McLean near the touchline and McLean's pal Billy Dickson, no doubt seeing himself as his little friend's guardian, went for the Rangers player. All hell broke loose with players pushing and shoving. Stein and Dickson were eventually sent off, and others who had become involved might well have gone too. Stein's dismissal, his third in just over a year, was greeted by a hail of bottles and cans and a chorus of obscenities from the visiting fans, and the police had to move into the crowd to restore order. After the resumption no further scoring took place. Despite the trouble the match left the 32,893 fans limp with excitement. It was an all-action, fast and furious contest, the second meeting of the teams this season and the second 3-3 draw. When last had a team come back to equalise three times against Rangers? Tommy McLean was the outstanding player on the field, a constant thorn in Rangers' side. Little wonder they signed him a little over two years later.

Kilmarnock: McLaughlan, King, Dickson, Gilmour, McGrory, Beattie, T. McLean, Queen, Morrison, J. McLean, McIlroy. Sub not used: McFadzean.

Rangers: Martin, Johansen, Mathieson, Greig, McKinnon, Watson, Henderson, Penman, Stein, Johnston, Persson (Jardine).

Kilmarnock v. Ayr United

Date: 30 October 1976   **Match title:** Scottish League Premier Division
Location: Rugby Park

This was only the second season of the Scottish League Premier Division. A ten-team set-up had replaced the old eighteen-team Division One, and the Ayrshire rivals Kilmarnock and Ayr United were meeting for the first time ever in a Premier Division match. Most people anticipated a close encounter, but in the event the match was anything but that.

Kilmarnock had recently transferred stalwart centre half Brian Rodman to Ayr United and he must have bitterly regretted his move after the events of this momentous afternoon as his former club produced a magnificent display of attacking football. Astonishingly, Killie had not yet won a League match, although they had beaten Ayr United 2-0 in a League Cup game in August.

With only eleven minutes played the home team took the lead. Davie Provan, a future Scottish international and a worthy successor to the great Tommy McLean on Killie's right wing, beat Ayr full-back Willie Kelly twice and crossed perfectly for Ronnie Sheed to head a fine goal. Three minutes later Killie's other winger Gordon Smith (still remembered for his late chance for Brighton in the 1983 FA Cup final) received a long ball from Billy Murdoch and danced past two opponents before crossing from the left for big Derrick McDicken to head over the despairing Andy Geoghegan. Sheed then had a chance after a defensive slip let him in, but he shot straight at the 'keeper and moments later, with the Ayr defence all at sea, another shot was kicked off the line. On thirty minutes it was 3-0 when McDicken headed the ball on to Ian Fallis to allow the striker to hit an angled shot across the goalkeeper into the net from around fifteen yards. The former Aberdeen 'keeper could not have been happy with himself over this one. The fourth goal in the thirty-fourth minute was the result of another defensive blunder that ended with a Fallis shot going in off a post.

Within minutes of referee T.R. Kyle of Glasgow starting the second half, Smith hit the bar and then Fallis shot wide when it looked easier to score, but the Killie centre forward completed his hat-trick in the fifty-fourth minute. Provan outwitted Kelly again and crossed beyond the goalkeeper for Fallis to head in, although the last touch may have come off Ayr defender Joe Filippi. Since around the twentieth minute Killie 'keeper Jim Stewart had been a virtual spectator, but early in the second half he at last had some work to do, and he twice produced fine saves, in particular one from Malcolm Robertson. Ayr manager Alex Stuart brought on his two permitted substitutes – powerful strikers Alex Ingram and Danny Masterton (on his debut) came on in place of the skilful Davie McCulloch and big Walker McCall, and for a time this undoubtedly improved matters for the Somerset Park team. With fifteen minutes left Kilmarnock brought on George Maxwell for Sheed, just in time for him to see Fallis run through the visitors defence but shoot straight at Geoghegan. Two minutes from time, as Killie stroked the ball about and with most of the away fans in the 7,600 crowd long gone, Ayr scored, and it was their two substitutes who did it. Ingram came in from the right and his cross was knocked into the net by Masterton. Their joy was short-lived, as this was just the spur Killie needed, and they went straight back up the field and Provan jinked through to cross

---

Kilmarnock 6
Sheed, McDicken
Fallis (3), Murdoch

         Ayr United 1
         Masterton

for Billy Murdoch (younger brother of Lisbon Lion Bobby) to head the final goal in Killie's 6-1 victory.

Kilmarnock had been in control of this match almost from start to finish and the score in no way exaggerated their supremacy on the day. It was the wingers, Provan in particular, and Smith who had destroyed the Ayr defence, who were simply unable to cope with their skill, pace, trickery and most of all crossing ability. Other top Killie men were Murdoch, McDicken and three-goal man Fallis. Manager Willie Fernie's belief in getting his team to play skilful, attacking football had won the day, although unfortunately this was not always to be the case. For Ayr's Geoghegan, Kelly and Rodman the game had been a nightmare, particularly with crosses, and a day they would wish to forget. McSherry, McDonald and the two substitutes were their best men. The result moved Kilmarnock above Ayr United in the League table. Sadly, within less than a year, the hat-trick scorer Ian Fallis, an amateur international signed from Queens Park in 1974, was killed in a road accident aged only twenty-three, on 3 October 1977.

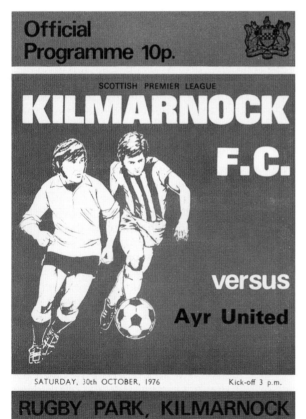

A programme for the Kilmarnock v. Ayr game, 1976.

Kilmarnock: Stewart, McLean, Robertson, Murdoch, Clarke, Welsh, Provan, McDicken, Fallis, Sheed (Maxwell), Smith. Sub not used: Sharp.

Ayr United: Geoghegan, McDonald, Kelly, Fleming, Rodman, Filippi, McSherry, Reid, McCall (Masterton), McCulloch (Ingram), M. Robertson.

KILMARNOCK v. CELTIC

Date: 6 March 1978   **Match title:** Scottish Cup Fourth Round Replay
Location: Rugby Park

Relegation from the Premier Division in 1977 was a huge blow to Kilmarnock and left the club facing financial difficulties. The problems were only partially eased by the transfer of Gordon Smith to Rangers for a fee of around £65,000. Before 1978 was out several other fine players would be on their way to more wealthy outfits. The club had already reverted to part-time football as a cost-cutting measure, but the decline since winning the Championship in 1965 was enormous.

The Scottish Cup provided Killie with an opportunity to raise morale and perhaps pick up some much-needed finance if they could draw attractive opposition. In the third round they drew St Mirren, then going well in the Premier Division under manager Alex Ferguson. The tie was away from home and underdogs Killie created a surprise by going to Love Street and winning 2-1 in front of a reasonable crowd of around 10,000. The fourth-round draw provided just what Kilmarnock needed: an away match against Celtic. They went to Parkhead without any great expectations of victory and probably surprised even themselves by holding Celtic to a 1-1 draw. Celtic's equaliser came with only six minutes left. When the teams reassembled at Rugby Park before a crowd of 14,137, both were already aware that the winners would face Rangers at Ibrox in the next round. Celtic had not been knocked out of the Scottish Cup by a team from a lower division since Dundee United did the trick in January 1949.

Early on Kilmarnock, in unfamiliar red and white stripes, made the running on a rainy, windswept night and indeed they pressurised Celtic for most of the first half. Young Davie Provan on Killie's right wing tortured opposing full-back John Dowie, going past him repeatedly and sending over crosses to test goalkeeper Peter Latchford and his defenders, but fortunately for Celtic, Latchford was in top form. With only nine minutes gone, from a tantalising Provan cross, Iain McCulloch, a midfield dynamo for Killie, swept the ball into the Celtic net, but referee A. McGunnigle from Glasgow ruled it out for some pushing by Colin Stein (on loan from Rangers since the tragic death of Ian Fallis in October). Jim Stewart in the Kilmarnock goal was also in excellent form, holding a long-range George McCluskey shot and then doing brilliantly to tip over a well-placed Roy Aitken header that was dipping under the bar. McCulloch was proving to be almost as much of a thorn in Celtic's side as Provan with his penetrating runs, and from one such run Aitken pulled him down in full flight and the Celtic captain was booked after thirty minutes. The home side continued their domination of the first half, but the teams went in at the interval locked at 0-0.

The Parkhead team began the second half much more convincingly and created three chances inside the first five minutes. Alan Robertson had to clear a Roddy MacDonald header off the line, then Tom McAdam ran through but scooped his shot weakly over the bar. Aitken then hit a blistering shot that Stewart pushed past the post. On fifty-seven minutes came what was probably the most significant moment of the match when Aitken floored Killie's George Maxwell, and having already been booked, he was ordered off. The tide now turned against Celtic and Donnie McDowell missed two clear-cut chances as Celtic once more found the

---

Kilmarnock 1   **Celtic 0**
McDicken

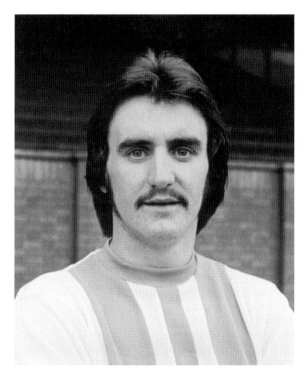

Scorer of the only goal of the game, big Derrick McDicken, who signed for Killie in 1972 and stayed until 1985, making 321 appearances and 24 as sub in League matches. He was best known as a central defender, but could play in a variety of positions.

pressure on them. Killie's Ian Jardine was booked for a foul on Tommy Burns, and then on seventy-seven minutes came an incredible one-handed save as Latchford pushed a vicious Stein shot over the bar. The home side brought on Jim Doherty for the out-of-touch McDowell, and with only eight minutes left were rewarded when towering defender Derrick McDicken came up for a corner. The Celtic defence only managed to clear it as far as 'Big D', and he lashed a low shot through a crowd of players and in off the post from around twenty-five yards out. It was Derrick's only goal of the season, but what a time to get it, and minutes later the same man was back in defence to clear a 'Shuggie' Edvaldsson shot off his own line. As the whistle sounded on a shock, but deserved victory, a large number of Killie's younger fans invaded the field to congratulate their heroes. The main targets for them would surely be Stewart, McDicken, McCulloch and of course Provan.

Five days later it was part-time Kilmarnock, and not Celtic, who made the trip to Ibrox for a quarter-final tie, and the tickets which had been printed in expectation of an 'Old Firm' clash had to be destroyed. Killie lost 4-1 to a Rangers side which went on to win the treble. As a further postscript it should be noted that in September, new Celtic manager Billy McNeil, who could not fail to have been impressed by Davie Provan's performances, signed him for Celtic for what was then a record transfer fee between Scottish clubs of £120,000.

Kilmarnock: Stewart, McLean, Robertson, Jardine, Clarke, McDicken, Provan, McDowell (Doherty), Stein, Maxwell, McCulloch. Sub not used: Murdoch.
Celtic: Latchford, Sneddon, Dowie, Filippi, MacDonald, Aitken, Edvaldsson, McAdam, McCluskey, Burns, Wilson. Subs not used: Craig, Casey.

RANGERS v. KILMARNOCK

Date: 5 August 1979   **Match title:** Tennent-Caledonian Cup Final
Location: Ibrox Park

Kilmarnock found themselves slightly surprised but nevertheless delighted to be invited to take part in Rangers' annual pre-season four-team tournament, the Tennent-Caledonian Cup, now into its fourth year. It was suggested that their invitation owed a lot to having created an excellent impression on the Ibrox hierarchy when they gave two fine displays against Rangers in the Scottish Cup in February before going down in a replay, and also to some terrific attacking performances during their promotion-winning League season of 1978/79. As in previous years the format of the tournament meant that two Scottish and two English sides would meet at Ibrox in two semi-finals, plus a final and a third-place play-off over a weekend. This year the two English clubs involved were West Ham and Brighton, both at the time in the top division in England. The draw paired Killie with Brighton on the Friday evening, and was followed immediately afterwards by Rangers against the Hammers. Kilmarnock drew 1-1 with Brighton – the highlight without doubt was a classic goal scored by the highly talented Ian Gibson, who skipped past two defenders, drew the 'keeper and slotted a perfect finish high into the net. Killie duly won the penalty shoot-out 6-5 to qualify for the final. As Rangers then beat West Ham 3-2 in the other game it was to be an all-Scottish final on the Sunday.

Davie Sneddon's men made it hard for themselves in the first half of the final. The Kilmarnock frontmen looked rather toothless as they squandered some good creative play by their midfield. Rangers, in the middle of a heavy pre-season fixture schedule although Killie's was almost as intense, were struggling to find reserves of energy as they tried to push forward, but neither side could find the net in a rather dull first half. Within four minutes of the restart Davie Cooper sent a through ball to Bobby Russell, and the midfield man raced to the byline and crossed to the far post where ex-Killie player Gordon Smith netted with a flying header. Then, with fifty-eight minutes played, it seemed all over when the gifted Cooper shrugged off several tackles inside the box and laid the ball back for Ally Dawson to thump a thunderous shot past the helpless Alan McCulloch from around twelve yards. Rangers were now coasting, it seemed, but the problem was that they were running out of steam. Derek Parlane was brought on to replace Derek Johnstone, and young Steven Richardson came on for Sandy Jardine who had taken a thigh knock. Then came the stunning finale as victory was snatched from the jaws of defeat. Killie threw everything at the struggling Ibrox team and were finally rewarded with only four minutes left when Bobby Street hammered home a fine McDicken pass. Could Rangers hold on? Goalkeeper Peter McCloy was performing small miracles as Rangers panicked, but in the last minute Kilmarnock forced another corner, which was played in towards the near post. The ball actually hit the post and an almighty scramble took place with Rangers full-back Alex Miller somehow contriving to handle the ball on the line to stop his own header going in. Referee Ian Foote immediately pointed to the spot, and with the game now entering injury time, up stepped Killie's reliable penalty-kick expert George Maxwell to slot it away. Rangers had been preparing to lift the trophy, and it had been snatched from their grasp by

Rangers 2	Kilmarnock 2
Smith	*Street*
Dawson	*Maxwell (pen)*

a last-gasp all-out effort. Extra time was not an option in this tournament; it was straight to penalty kicks. Jimmy Hughes, who had come on as a substitute, netted the first Killie kick, and Kenny Watson did likewise for Rangers. Then Stuart McLean and Gordon Smith made it 2-2, Ian Jardine and Alex Miller respectively made it 3-3. Bobby Street netted Killie's fourth penalty, but then, crucially, Davie Cooper's kick was saved by Alan McCulloch's feet, meaning that if the visitors could score with their fifth penalty kick, victory would be theirs. So for the second time George Maxwell stepped up, having netted his kick in the last minute of the game. Could he now win it with another penalty? Of course he could, and his team-mates charged out from the centre-circle to greet him as the ball hit the net. Killie walked off with the cup and the champagne as their supporters went into ecstasy. A large number of the crowd had actually missed the late drama in this match as they had left with Rangers two goals ahead and seemingly cruising to inevitable victory. There must have a lot of shocked Rangers fans when their mates who had stayed on till the end got back to the pub and informed them of the outcome. For the record, Brighton beat West Ham 3-1 in the third-place match, and the Tennent-Caledonian Cup was never played for again. Thus Kilmarnock were the last-ever winners.

Captain Alan Robertson, surrounded by team-mates, holds up the Tennent-Caledonian Cup. Clockwise from Robertson are K. Armstrong, A. Mauchlen, S. McLean, R .Street, J. Hughes, I. Jardine, P. Clarke, A. McCulloch, J. Brown.

Rangers: McCloy, Miller, Dawson, Jardine (Richardson), Jackson, Watson, McLean, Russell, Johnstone (Parlane), Smith, Cooper. Subs not used: A. MacDonald, J. MacDonald, Kennedy.
Kilmarnock: McCulloch, McLean, Robertson, Jardine, Clarke, McDicken, Gibson (Doherty), Maxwell, Bourke (Hughes), Mauchlen, Street. Subs not used: Brown, Welsh, Armstrong.

Queen of the South v. Kilmarnock

Date: 13 May 1989   **Match title:** Scottish League First Division
Location: Palmerston Park, Dumfries

Kilmarnock travelled to play Queen of the South on the last day of the season facing the prospect of being relegated from the First Division to the Second Division. They had lost 3-2 at Clydebank the previous Saturday after being ahead 2-0 and were second from bottom, behind third-bottom Clyde on goal difference. Killie's goal difference was -19, while Clyde's was -14. However, Killie's opponents Queen of the South were bottom of the League and long since relegated, so it was felt that the opportunity was there to score a few goals and perhaps get above Clyde, who were at home to St Johnstone that afternoon. Any victory margin at all would be sufficient to spare Kilmarnock the humiliation of relegation if Clyde failed to win against the Perth Saints.

A reasonable estimate of those in attendance would be that eighty per cent of them were Kilmarnock supporters – it was clear that many Queens fans had given up on their team for this season. Despite going straight into attack from the kick-off, it took Killie until the thirty-ninth minute to score when the legendary dumpy little goal-grabber Willie Watters cashed in on Gary Fraser's suicidal backpass to his goalkeeper Willie Cunningham. For all their pressure this was the only goal in the first half, but the Killie fans were not too unhappy when their radios relayed the fact that Clyde were drawing 0-0 in their game, and if things were to remain as they were Killie would be safe from the drop. However, on forty-seven minutes things got even better when Colin Harkness burst down the right wing and sent in a cross which deceived the goalkeeper, hit the bar and fell to Watters, who fired it into the net through Cunningham's legs. On fifty-four minutes the little carpet-fitter completed his hat-trick. He sprinted fifteen yards with the ball, not really Willie's forte, went past Mark Shanks and struck it home. With sixty-one minutes played Robert Reilly broke the Watters scoring sequence by getting in on the act after a fine solo run left him with a simple finish. The home defence was now in danger of disintegrating altogether, and on sixty-nine minutes Watters got his fourth and Killie's fifth when he capitalised on John Gamble's curious hesitancy in clearing when the ball was in the danger area. Tempers were becoming a bit frayed and Queens' ex-Killie player Tom McDonald was sent off for a bad foul on Reilly, and then Derek Cook was booked. Late on Watters netted yet again, but was adjudged offside, and then word came through on the radios around the ground that Clyde were ahead by 1-0 and that Killie's five goals were not enough, one more was needed. With three minutes left Willie Watters broke away and scored his fifth, and Killie finished the game 6-0 winners. The fans were overjoyed.

Meanwhile, the radio news from Firhill in Glasgow, where Clyde were playing their home games at this time, was that Clyde were only 1-0 ahead, giving Kilmarnock the advantage with goal difference level, as the Rugby Parkers had scored 8 goals more than Clyde. When the final whistle sounded at Palmerston the delirious Killie fans invaded the field to celebrate, and the area in front of the main stand became a sea of blue and white scarves. Fans sang and cheered for almost ten minutes and the atmosphere was electric. The vastly outnumbered police and stewards stood back and allowed the happy fans to enjoy their celebrations. Only

Queen of the South 0	Kilmarnock 6
	Watters (5)
	Reilly

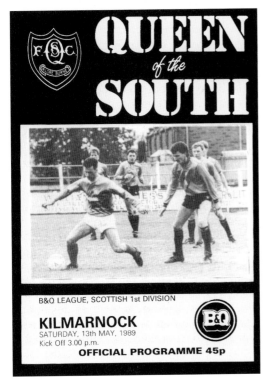

A programme for the match between Queen of the South and Kilmarnock, 1989.

one thing was missing – confirmation of the final score from Firhill! And then eventually it came, almost as if the radio presenters were reluctant to break the news and break hearts, it had taken so long. In the ninety-seventh minute Clyde had been awarded a penalty kick, and McGlashan had converted it to make the final result 2-0 and put Clyde back ahead by one solitary goal on goal difference. A hush came over the fans as word was passed around, many not believing or not wanting to believe the message. Many of the previously ecstatic supporters trudged away in tears, and made the sad journey home unable to comprehend that they had won 6-0 away from home but were still relegated by one goal on goal difference. It was rough justice and the final irony was that apparently the referee at Firhill had added on so much time because of time-wasting by the Clyde players, who were trying to protect their 1-0 lead, unaware of the extent of Killie's second-half goal spree! Further irony lay in the fact that had Queens conceded one more goal, not only would Kilmarnock have stayed up, but it would have been the 100th League goal conceded by the Dumfries team that season. The new regime, led by Bobby Fleeting, desperately trying to gain control at Rugby Park at the time, ultimately successfully, would have to commence their rebuilding work in the Scottish League Second Division.

Queen of the South: Cunningham, Shanks, Sim, Mills, Gamble, Fraser, Docherty, McDonald, Stewart (Telfer), Cook, Sloan.
Kilmarnock: McCulloch, Montgomerie, McLean, MacFarlane (Derek Walker), Marshall, Flexney, Davidson, Watters, Harkness (McLaughlin), Reilly, Stewart.

RANGERS v. KILMARNOCK

Date: 28 August 1993
Location: Ibrox Park

Match title: Scottish League Premier Division

After an absence of ten years Kilmarnock FC returned to the Premier Division in 1993. Under the shrewd management of Tommy Burns, and with fairly substantial financial investment that allowed the return of full-time football, Killie had improved vastly during the previous three years and morale, both on the field and among the fans, was at an extremely high level. The first Premier Division match, against Dundee, had been won, but the next two were lost and the fourth fixture was against Rangers at Ibrox, easily the biggest test so far. Rangers, League Champions for each of the last five seasons, had also won the treble in the previous season and had not lost at home in 32 games over the last seventeen months. What chance did newly promoted Killie have?

Kilmarnock sold out their full allocation of 3,600 tickets and their fans, packed behind the goal at the Broomloan Stand end, released hundreds of blue and white balloons as the players took the field on a beautiful day. For some time after kick-off, players were still trying to negotiate their way around the last remnants of the sea of balloons. With only three minutes gone Gus MacPherson needlessly gave away a corner from Gary Stevens' high cross, and from the resultant kick Neil Murray's low shot forced Bobby Geddes into a fine save. Minutes later the 'keeper was again in action to stop Davie Robertson's right-foot effort. However, it was not all one way, and Killie settled and began showing the 44,243 crowd what they were capable of when Bobby Williamson went on a run and slipped the ball left to Shaun McSkimming, who struck a powerful left-foot shot which Ally Maxwell managed to hold. Rangers' main weapons in attack were the tall strikers Mark Hateley and Duncan Ferguson, and Killie found themselves increasingly under pressure from high balls into the box, but although Killie's two central defenders Ray Montgomerie and Andy Millen were giving away 5 or 6ins in height to their direct opponents, they seemed to be able to cope with everything thrown at them with surprising ease. As the game wore on, and Kilmarnock showing no sign of wilting, the home fans and some of the Rangers players became frustrated at this unexpected turn of events. On thirty-five minutes Kilmarnock created another good chance when George McCluskey touched the ball back to Ally Mitchell, and the winger hit a low shot from around twenty-two yards, but Maxwell got down well to touch it past for a corner. Half-time came with the score at 0-0, but it had been far from a backs-to-the-wall performance from Killie. They had almost as much of the play as the home side and their fans were delighted by the performance.

Early in the second half, Duncan Ferguson, for almost the first time, got away from his marker and cut in to strike a low shot off the base of the post, the nearest thing so far. Then with sixty-two minutes gone came the breakthrough, and it was the visitors who made it. McSkimming, who had given England international Stevens a difficult afternoon, wriggled his way past the full-back, and just a few yards from the byline, managed to get in a cross which waif-like seventeen-year-old Mark Roberts, in for the injured Mark Reilly, threw himself full-length at to head into the net, despite a despairing touch from 'keeper Maxwell. The Kilmarnock fans, packed behind that goal, went simply potty! It was Roberts' first goal for the first

---

Rangers 1
Pressley

Kilmarnock 2
Roberts
Williamson

Seventeen-year-old Mark Roberts, white shirt, on ground, dives to head the first goal in the 2-1 win at Ibrox, right in front of the Killie fans.

team, and what a time and place to get it. Soon after, Mitchell had a chance to make it two when Murray's badly hit pass went straight to him inside the box, but Ally sliced his shot badly. Naturally Rangers came storming back, and on seventy-two minutes forced an equaliser when, from substitute Ian Durrant's cross from the left, Steven Pressley got to the high ball before Geddes and his header dropped into the empty net. Rangers were now expected to go on and take the points, but it simply did not happen. Sure they pressed, still using high balls, but Killie would not yield. The match was held up for around three minutes to allow referee Ian Taylor of Edinburgh to receive treatment from the Killie physio, and it was with the game dragging on well into time added on for this injury that the climax unfolded. MacPherson chipped the ball down the right wing deep into Rangers territory, hoping to kill some time. Killie substitute Tom Brown, who had come on along with Ian Porteous just minutes before, got possession ahead of Pressley, who had been trying to let it run out for a goal kick. Brown turned it back to Porteous, Porteous shot, Maxwell could only parry it and the ball ran free for the incoming Bobby Williamson to knock it over the line for one of the simplest goals of his career. Simple it may have been, but to say the fans behind the goal went completely mad would be an understatement. Two minutes later the final whistle sounded on a result that caused shockwaves throughout Scotland and announced to everyone that Kilmarnock Football Club was back!

Rangers: Maxwell, Stevens, Gough, Pressley, Robertson, Steven, Murray, I. Ferguson, Mikhailichenko, D. Ferguson (Durrant), Hateley. Subs not used: Wishart, Scott.
Kilmarnock: Geddes, MacPherson, Montgomerie, Millen, Black, Mitchell, Skilling, Roberts (Porteous), McSkimming, McCluskey (Brown), Williamson. Sub not used: Matthews.

KILMARNOCK v. RANGERS

Date: 7 May 1994   **Match title:** Scottish League Premier Division
Location: Rugby Park

Kilmarnock had proven the critics wrong with persistent battling performances throughout the 1993/94 campaign. Nevertheless, with only 2 matches remaining, the relegation issue was far from settled. Three clubs were to be relegated this season (and only one promoted) in order to reduce the Premier Division back to ten clubs. Raith Rovers and Dundee were already down, but any one of four others (Partick Thistle, Hearts, St Johnstone or Kilmarnock) could still accompany them. At this point Killie had 2 points less than Partick and 1 less than the other two. The second to last fixture was a home game against Rangers – not exactly the match they would have chosen. Quite apart from the relegation issue and the fact that the opposition was the Champions, further importance was lent to this potential blockbuster of a match by the fact that Rugby Park was hosting its last ever match in its present form. The following day the bulldozers would be moving in to demolish the terracing to allow the construction of a new all-seated stadium with a capacity of just over 18,000. This simultaneous occurrence of significant events evoked memories of the Killie v. Celtic game of August 1899, if anyone was still around from those days to recall it! The most important thing in 1994 was that Killie took something from this game against Rangers to ensure that when the new stadium was complete it was staging Premier Division football.

Manager Tommy Burns decided that experience would be vital and chose to include both himself and his player/assistant manager Billy Stark in the line-up. With only seven minutes gone Rangers' Alexei Mikhailichenko broke away on the left, laid the ball across in front of Charlie Miller, and watched in horror as the youngster side-footed the ball high over the bar from eight yards. Soon it was Killie's turn to attack, and McSkimming on the byline turned the ball back for Gus MacPherson to cross from the right wing to Billy Stark who volleyed it over the bar. Then a short corner kick by Mark Reilly to Tom Black produced a fine cross which Burns headed powerfully for goal, only for Colin Scott to hold well, and the game continued in an end-to-end fashion until the interval came with the score 0-0.

When the game resumed Killie had replaced the injured Bobby Williamson with Tom Brown, and within minutes the substitute received a chipped pass from Burns and slipped the ball to McSkimming. He crossed for McCluskey to force Scott into another diving save from his glancing header. Then came perhaps the best chance of the match – Rangers right-back Fraser Wishart received a pass from Mark Hateley, made ground down the right and put in a low cross to Ally McCoist, but the usually deadly Ally knocked a great chance over the bar. On sixty-four minutes Killie were awarded a free-kick about twenty-five yards out near the corner of Rangers' penalty area. The kick was touched short for Tom Black to shoot hard and low, but Scott did well to get down and smother the ball at the foot of his left-hand post. On seventy-three minutes Killie had their most clear-cut opportunity so far. Stark showed great vision to slide a pass through to release Andy Millen to run clean through on his own with only 'keeper Scott between him and the goal. Unfortunately, magnificent defender that Andy undoubtedly was, he was probably not the man you would choose for such a situation, but he did look cool as he

Kilmarnock 1   **Rangers 0**
  Black

A lavish special edition of the club programme was produced for the last match before the re-building of the stadium.

slipped the ball past Scott and inches past the left-hand post! Andy and most of his colleagues fell to their knees and the Killie fans held their heads in their hands. Would Killie live to regret this miss? With seventy-nine minutes gone the home side got another free-kick in a very similar position to the one Black had taken a free-kick from fourteen minutes earlier, perhaps a couple of yards further back. MacPherson touched the kick short to Black, and he hit an even better low left-foot rocket, again right down at Scott's left-hand post, but this time the 'keeper could not quite get there quickly enough, and Black's shot thudded low into the net to spark joyous celebrations. Hateley then moved back up front as Rangers chased an equaliser, but Killie held out fairly comfortably, with Ray Montgomerie inspirational in defence, just as Burns and Stark had been, pulling the strings in midfield. Just before the end the fans received more good news on their radios – Aberdeen had scored against St Johnstone, and defeat for the Saints dropped them into the third-bottom spot. When referee W. Morrison of Carluke blew his whistle for full-time, the home fans in the 18,012 crowd exploded in relief and joy. Their team had fought like tigers and deserved the points for their tremendous effort.

The following week Killie travelled, along with over 6,000 fans, to Edinburgh for the final League match and easily held Hibs, who never looked like scoring, to a goal-less draw, which was enough to ensure survival in the Premier Division after a gruelling 44-game programme.

Kilmarnock: Geddes, MacPherson, Black, Montgomerie, Burns, Millen, Stark, Reilly, Williamson (Brown), McCluskey, McSkimming. Subs not used: Meldrum, Napier.
Rangers: Scott, Wishart, Gough, Hateley, Robertson, Durrant (Huistra), Murray, Kuznetsov, Mikhailichenko, C. Miller (Hagen), McCoist. Sub not used: Inglis.

KILMARNOCK v. FALKIRK

Date: 24 May 1997   **Match title:** Tennents Scottish Cup Final
Location: Ibrox Park

For the eighth time, and the first since 1960, Kilmarnock reached the Scottish Cup final after defeating Dundee United in a replay at Easter Road. Hampden Park was being reconstructed at the time, so the final was played at Ibrox. The delighted Killie fans could not have cared less – most would have travelled to the moon to see their team in this match against Falkirk. First Division club or not, the Bairns had to be taken seriously, as they had beaten Celtic in a semi-final replay at Ibrox. Further spice was added by the fact that Falkirk were now managed by Alex Totten, who until December 1996 had been Killie's manager, but a run of poor results had seen him removed. His successor at Kilmarnock was Bobby Williamson, in his first managerial job. Falkirk were competing in only their third Scottish Cup final, but interestingly their previous appearance in 1957 had been against Killie, when they won 2-1 after a 1-1 draw.

On a beautiful day the teams ran out in front of an all-ticket crowd of 48,953, with one half of the ground decked out in the dark blue of Falkirk and the other half in the lighter blue of Killie. In the early stages Kilmarnock were very impressive and looked every inch the team from a higher division, finding team-mates consistently with their passes and generally looking much more threatening than Falkirk. The Bairns' main tactic, indeed it seemed their only tactic, was to have Andy Gray (who had played for Crystal Palace in the 1990 FA Cup final) throw the ball prodigious distances to the head of 6ft 7ins Kevin James. Without doubt this combination caused Kilmarnock problems on occasions, but on the whole they managed to nullify the threat, mainly due to the superb Kevin McGowne, a mere 6ft 2ins.

After twenty-one minutes of play, largely dominated by Killie, James headed the ball behind his own goal for a corner kick on Killie's right wing. Nineteen-year-old Alex Burke swung the ball over with his left foot towards McGowne, near the corner of the six-yard box. Kevin jumped high along with two Falkirk players, and the ball was glanced on by a head to where Paul Wright was lurking unmarked, and he struck a right-foot shot on the turn low into the right-hand corner of Craig Nelson's goal. Wright, Killie's top scorer, was a major doubt for this match – it was his first game for three weeks, having had thirteen stitches inserted in a knee wound after a horrendous tackle at Dunfermline. Twenty-five thousand Kilmarnock fans inside the ground were mighty glad that Paul had made it in time for this game.

With thirty-five minutes played came one of the best moves of the match. Falkirk's David Hagen flew down the right wing and sent over an exquisite right-foot cross to the back post, which evaded the defence and found the incoming Paul McGrillen, who had a great chance for the equaliser. However McGrillen, whose goal knocked out Celtic in the semi-final, got the wrong angle on his header and sent it back across and past Dragoje Lekovic's left-hand post. They would never have a better chance. Referee Hugh Dallas ended the first half with Killie a goal ahead.

Falkirk came out determined to improve on their first-half display and almost immediately Kevin McAllister had a shot knocked away for a corner. Then, on forty-nine minutes, Killie's Jim McIntyre had a chance, but his header lacked power and

---

Kilmarnock 1
   Wright

                              Falkirk 0

Alex Burke shoots for goal in the cup final as Dylan Kerr tries to get out of the way.

Nelson saved. Around the hour mark came the first two bookings for Dylan Kerr and goalscorer Wright, for tackles of which Mr Dallas disapproved. Then Killie missed a chance to tie-up the game. Wright, just inside his own half, controlled the ball beautifully and slipped a superb pass through for McIntyre to run onto clear of the defence, but as he got within shooting range he delayed, enabling Gray to get back to make a fine saving tackle. Then Scott Crabbe was booked, and Falkirk made the first change with Fellner coming on for McGrillen. Killie's McGowne had to leave the field for treatment to a head wound, and Gary Holt filled in for him at the back until he returned heavily bandaged. Lekovic then produced a wonderful save from a James header that was going in at the top left-hand corner. Killie spurned another chance of a clincher on seventy-five minutes when MacPherson slipped the ball inside the full-back for Burke to run onto, but Nelson blocked Burke's left-foot shot. John Henry came on for the tiring Wright on seventy-seven minutes. Then on eighty-five minutes came controversy, when yet another long throw from Gray was headed on by James and Neil Oliver hooked it into the net, but the linesman's flag was immediately up for offside and the Killie fans breathed again. Just before the end Gray levelled up the bookings with a foul on Killie substitute Brown, and Falkirk's last chance went when Fellner shot high over seconds before the final whistle. Kilmarnock had won the Scottish Cup for the third time.

Despite their obvious disappointment, it was magnificent to see the Falkirk fans stay to clap Ray Montgomerie and his Killie players as they took the cup round to the Falkirk end to mutual applause. It had indeed been the 'Friendly Final'.

Kilmarnock: Lekovic, MacPherson, D. Kerr, Montgomerie, McGowne, Reilly, Bagan (Mitchell), Holt, Wright (Henry), McIntyre (Brown), Burke.
Falkirk: Nelson, McGowan, Seaton, Oliver, James, Gray, McAllister, McKenzie, Crabbe (Craig), Hagen, McGrillen (Fellner). Sub not used: Mathers.

DUNFERMLINE v. KILMARNOCK

Date: 17 April 1999   **Match title:** Scottish Premier League
Location: East End Park, Dunfermline

Season 1998/99 was Kilmarnock's best since their return to the Premier Division in 1993. They held second place from September until February, and although they had now dropped to third place behind Celtic, they were still fairly certain of qualifying for a place in European football when they visited Dunfermline to play a team who were struggling to avoid relegation from the top ten. Kilmarnock had already won 3-0 at East End Park back in November when Ian Durrant had inspired the team, and as a bonus had scored his first two goals as a Kilmarnock player. For this second visit in April Killie manager Bobby Williamson sprang a slight surprise by recalling his mercurial French striker Jerome Vareille, who had been out injured since December, and it was a move that was to pay off handsomely.

Dunfermline were under pressure almost from the first minute, and it was comeback man Vareille who was first to threaten when he cracked in a right-foot shot that goalkeeper Lee Butler did well to hold. In the twenty-sixth minute Killie opened the scoring. Alan Mahood crossed in a low ball from the right and John Henry at the near post cracked it low just inside Butler's left-hand post from around six yards out. Killie maestro Ian Durrant was controlling the midfield, but it was Dunfermline's Scott Thomson who nearly equalised on thirty-six minutes, but Jim Lauchlan saved the day with a brave diving header, and then a minute before half-time Gordon Marshall was forced to touch away a looping Andy Tod header which would have gone in just under the bar. Despite their superior passing skills Kilmarnock went in at half-time only 1-0 ahead, and the match was still undecided.

Dunfermline manager Dick Campbell sent on striker Andy Smith and took off defender Richard Huxford in an attempt to grab a leveller, but it was to backfire spectacularly in the second half as the Pars committed themselves forward and were destroyed by Killie's slick passing when they broke upfield. On fifty-five minutes Gus MacPherson floated a pass to Vareille on the right, Vareille crossed and Henry had shots blocked twice before the ball broke back for Ally Mitchell to knock it in with his left foot, helped by a ricochet off Dunfermline's Marc Millar. Killie turned up the heat and the Pars had no answer. Three minutes later Millar lost possession thirty-five yards from his own goal, Durrant picked it up and ran through to slot a majestic shot past the helpless Butler to make it 3-0. Kilmarnock were now firing on all cylinders and so completely in charge that many of the Dunfermline fans were already heading out of the ground with half an hour still left. On sixty-eight minutes came the outstanding goal of the game. A great seven-man passing movement put Vareille clear on the right, and he cut in and unleashed a thunderbolt of a shot that 'keeper Butler hardly saw as it flew high into the rigging. Number five followed on seventy-five minutes after another slick passing move was completed by Mahood sliding the ball across to the unmarked Henry, who had time to take it under control and shoot high into Butler's top right-hand corner from twenty yards for his second goal. Around this time Killie were able to display their attacking options as they made three substitutions, putting on Gary

---

Dunfermline 0   **Kilmarnock 6**
                                     Henry (2), Mitchell
                                     Durrant, Vareille, McCoist

McCutcheon, Ally McCoist and Paul Wright for Vareille, Mitchell and Durrant respectively. A great day out for the Killie fans was made complete in the last minute when Killie 'keeper Gordon Marshall took a goal kick and from there no Dunfermline player touched the ball until it hit their net, courtesy of substitute Ally McCoist who had run onto a lobbed pass from Henry and banged it past the 'keeper. Much hilarity, at least among the visiting supporters, followed when Ally stood to attention, saluted and waited as his team-mates came up to shake hands in a very formal manner as Ally bowed to each one in turn. It was typical Ally showmanship. This was a fantastic display by a Kilmarnock side that just clicked, as everyone seemed to be on their best form and the passing had been especially sharp and accurate. Durrant was the Man of the Match, but Marshall, MacPherson, Mahood and Henry had also starred in a team that looked to be superior to their opponents in every department. In the end Killie managed to qualify for Europe, but the Pars were sadly relegated. The damage done to their morale by the result on this afternoon could not have helped their cause in any way.

Ian Durrant, with hand raised, has just netted Killie's third goal against Dunfermline.

Dunfermline: Butler, Millar (Squires), Shields, Tod, Huxford (A. Smith), Thomson, Dair, Dolan, Petrie, Graham (Nish), Coyle.
Kilmarnock: Marshall, MacPherson, Innes, Lauchlan, D. Kerr, Mahood, Durrant (Wright), Reilly, Henry, Mitchell (McCoist), Vareille (McCutcheon).

RANGERS v. KILMARNOCK

Date: 28 October 2000
Location: Ibrox Park

Match title: Scottish Premier League

Kilmarnock visited Ibrox in a confident mood having been unbeaten in ten matches. They actually had a point more than their opponents, although Rangers had played a game less. There was no denying that Rangers were going through a sticky patch; nevertheless the bookmakers were quoting a Killie victory at 7-1, or even in one case, 9-1 against. Many Kilmarnock fans were quick to take advantage of what they saw as extremely attractive odds given their team's excellent recent form. Killie, playing in their change strip of navy blue with burgundy trim, reintroduced former French International Christophe Cocard to the side for his first start since August, against a Rangers side who, despite recent poor form, were unbeaten in the last 20 home games.

As expected Rangers quickly went on the offensive, and inside the first few minutes Killie's Chris Innes had to make a fine last-ditch challenge to stop Rod Wallace connecting with an Andrei Kanchelskis cross. With five minutes played Freddie Dindeleux fed the ball to Cocard, who played it left to Andy McLaren. McLaren returned it back across right into the path of the advancing Cocard who coolly side-footed the ball from around seven yards out past the helpless Christiansen. It was the Frenchman's first goal of the season, and even more remarkably he scored it while wearing trainers, as he had left his boots at Rugby Park and a fast car had been sent back to Kilmarnock to fetch them, but it had not yet returned! Soon after, a long-range shot from McLaren flew past Christiansen's left-hand post, and in Killie's next foray they cut open the Rangers defence, and McLaren attempted an audacious cross from the left using the outside of his right foot, but the 'keeper intercepted it. Fernando Ricksen and Alan Mahood squared-up after a clash, Ian Durrant pushed Ricksen away and then Sergio Porrini got involved as Durrant clearly indicated that Ricksen had dived. The outcome was a free-kick to the home side which was blocked by the Killie wall. With thirty-two minutes played Durrant chipped a perfectly weighted through ball for Scottish international Gary Holt to run onto through the middle. Gary held off Arthur Numan's challenge and ran on to strike a low left-foot shot past Christiansen. Within minutes Cocard and McLaren again baffled the Rangers defence. McLaren slipped the ball through Lorenzo Amoruso's legs, raced into the box pursued by Tugay and Amoruso, and between them they brought him down, but no penalty was awarded, and to rub salt into McLaren's wound Tugay pushed his hand into the Killie man's face and escaped any punishment for that as well. Durrant and Mahood were dominating the midfield, ably assisted by the grafters Holt and Mitchell. With the Killie passing always very precise, Cocard and McLaren were a constant threat up front. However with thirty-eight minutes gone, Gary Hay pulled down Porrini just outside the box, but Ronald De Boer's free-kick struck the wall and went away for Rangers' first corner of the match. Seconds before the interval Kanchelskis had a chance, but he shot wildly off-target, and when referee John Underhill blew for half-time Killie still held a 2-0 lead and the majority of the 49,569 crowd were far from happy.

When the teams returned Billy Dodds had replaced Kanchelskis, and on fifty-three minutes Kenny Miller came on for Porrini, but although the home side spent more

---

Rangers 0

Kilmarnock 3
Cocard, Holt
Numan (og)

Gary Holt shrugs off Arthur Numan and then runs on to net Killie's second goal.

time in Killie's half, 'keeper Gordon Marshall had still not had to make a save. McLaren went on another mazy run and set up Mahood for a low right-foot shot that Christiansen stopped with a foot. Then De Boer crossed a good ball in from the right touchline and Marshall could not hold it, but it was scrambled away. Then when Bert Konterman failed to control the ball Mitchell took advantage and pushed it wide to McLaren, who struck a left-foot shot over the bar. On sixty-seven minutes the classy Dindeleux pushed forward into the Rangers half, knocked the ball right to Cocard who sent it back left to McLaren. Andy cut into the box and hit a hard low ball across the face of the goal intended for Cocard at the back post, but Numan intervened and the ball cannoned off him into the net for an own goal, and Ibrox began to empty rapidly.

Two minutes later Cocard went off and fellow countryman Jerome Vareille replaced him. Marshall was then called upon to block a Rod Wallace header, but Killie broke away again with some fine interpassing, and Vareille's twenty-five-yard shot was saved by Christiansen. He had another chance before the end when, following a poor kick-out by the 'keeper, Amoruso managed to block Vareille's shot. In the last minute Dindeleux blocked a powerful De Boer drive, and seconds later the game ended with Kilmarnock decisive 3-0 winners.

Killie had passed the ball superbly with their magnificent four-man midfield. While Innes and Dindeleux in central defence were also terrific, Marshall in goal could rarely have had an easier match.

Rangers: Christiansen, Porrini (Miller), Konterman, Amoruso, Numan, Ricksen, Tugay, McCann, Kanchelskis (Dodds), De Boer, Wallace (Adamczuk). Subs not used: Brown, Ross.
Kilmarnock: Marshall, MacPherson, Innes, Dindeleux, Hay, Holt, Mahood, Durrant (Fowler), Mitchell, Cocard (Vareille), McLaren (Dargo). Subs not used: Meldrum, Canning.

St Mirren v. Kilmarnock

Date: 6 February 2001
Location: Hampden Park
Match title: CIS Insurance League Cup Semi-Final

Kilmarnock qualified for the League Cup semi-final courtesy of victories over Clyde, St Johnstone and Hibernian. Their opponents were St Mirren, a team experiencing their first season in the Premier Division since 1991/92, and now fighting to avoid instant relegation back to the First Division. Kilmarnock were comfortably placed in fourth position, and had beaten the Saints in all three of the League meetings played earlier. Therefore they were hot favourites to win a place in the final. Unfortunately the weather was very unkind to the teams – the match was played on a terrible evening of driving wind and torrential rain, and this, combined with the live television coverage, kept the crowd down to only 9,213. Nevertheless, despite the low attendance, the fans who had turned up succeeded in creating a very lively atmosphere with almost constant singing and cheering; after all, it was the diehards that formed the majority of the crowd on such a night.

St Mirren, the underdogs, held their own in the early stages. Killie's McLaren had forced a corner inside the first two minutes when his cross was blocked, but then St Mirren's Scott MacKenzie had a shot which went over the bar, and Mark Yardley headed a long cross into the box just wide, all within the opening five minutes. Then on nine minutes, after a good run by Paul Rudden, Gary Bowman of Saints had a shooting chance, but Marshall easily saved his weak effort. Gradually though, Killie got to grips with the slippery pitch, and their passes began to find their intended targets instead of skidding away from them. Gus MacPherson lofted a ball into the box for Andy McLaren, but his downward header failed to create any problems for Ludovic Roy, and within two minutes MacPherson found himself booked for a rash challenge on Bowman. On eighteen minutes Killie's brave little striker Craig Dargo got an opportunity, but he snatched at it and his powerful right-foot shot flew over. Just three minutes later he had another more difficult chance which he attempted to lob over the goalkeeper, but the ball ended up in Roy's hands. Then MacPherson hit over an inviting cross, but no Killie player could get on the end of it. The Rugby Park team began to dominate, with full-back MacPherson particularly prominent as he continually popped up around the edge of the St Mirren penalty area. On twenty-five minutes McLaren cleverly clipped a corner kick to the lurking MacPherson in precisely that position, but Gus did not get a proper hold of this shot. Two minutes later the adventurous full-back had yet another shot well saved by Roy. Saints broke this spell of Killie domination when from a corner kick on thirty minutes, Yardley's looping back-header would have gone in had Ally Mitchell not headed it away. It was the closest St Mirren were to come all night. MacPherson, again up with the attack, had yet another shot from around twenty yards blocked, and then McLaren squandered an opportunity. With plenty of support up, he went for the shot, but sent the ball low past the far post. However, the strong suspicion that Killie would soon score proved correct five minutes before the interval when Paul Wright took possession out on the right wing, beat a man, and sent over a near-perfect cross towards McLaren, who judged his leap perfectly to get above Rudden and head powerfully past Roy from around six yards. A minute later

St Mirren 0

Kilmarnock 3
McLaren, Dargo
Canero

Mitchell was slightly late with his tackle on Rudden and was shown a yellow card. Few realised it at the time, perhaps not even Mitchell, but this minor infringement was to cause him to miss the final, as it was his second yellow card of the tournament.

Within five minutes of the start of the second half both teams had made claims for penalty kicks, but referee Kenny Clark turned down both, probably correctly. Saints then sent on the enigmatic Jose Quitongo in place of MacKenzie, and he produced a couple of typically mazy runs that ultimately bore no fruit, and Kilmarnock remained well in command of the situation. With sixty-eight minutes played came the outstanding moment of the game. A St Mirren corner was cleared out to Dargo, midway inside his own half, and he controlled the ball and set off on a lung-bursting run, chased by Saints substitute Hugh Murray. Dargo kept ahead of him and managed to evade two other defenders, until he got within a few yards of Saints' penalty area from where he unleashed a ferocious right-foot shot high into the net past the helpless Roy. It was Scotland's goal of the season, never mind goal of the match, and finished the game as a contest.

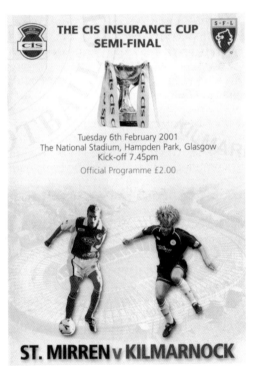

Left: Programme for the CIS Insurance Cup semi-final. *Right:* Gus MacPherson was an outstanding performer at right-back in this game.

St Mirren: Roy, Baltacha, Rudden, Turner, Walker, Bowman (Murray), Kerr, Gillies, MacKenzie (Quitongo), Fenton (McGarry), Yardley. Subs not used: Scrimgour, Nicolson.
Kilmarnock: Marshall, MacPherson, McGowne, Dindeleux, Baker, Canero, Holt, Mitchell (Reilly), McLaren, Wright (Cocard), Dargo (Fowler). Subs not used: Stewart, Hay.

Craig Dargo's amazing 'goal of the season' against St Mirren at Hampden.

As the Love Street team tried to come back Ricky Gillies shot high over the bar, and then they brought on Steven McGarry for Englishman Graham Fenton, but it made little difference. Kilmarnock had always looked to have more quality than the Saints, who rarely threatened a Rugby Park defence in which Kevin McGowne, in for the suspended Chris Innes, was a dominating figure. With seventy-eight minutes on the clock, McLaren hit a pinpoint free-kick from the right, Gary Holt beat 6'5" Sergei Baltacha (son of the Russian, and later Ukrainian international of the same name) in the air and nodded the ball down to young Peter Canero, who got his foot to the ball before Tommy Turner and stabbed it low into the net for his first goal for the club and to complete a comprehensive 3-0 win for Kilmarnock. With all doubts removed, Killie then brought on Mark Reilly and James Fowler for goal-hero Dargo and the hardworking Mitchell, and were content to play out time. Gus MacPherson managed to get in one more flashing right-foot shot a few minutes from the end, but he could not quite manage to get his name on the scoresheet, despite his repeated valiant attempts. He had given a remarkable performance, but the Man of the Match award had to go to Craig Dargo, playing his first-ever game at the National Stadium. When receiving his award he admitted that it had been the best goal he had ever scored, and all those who saw it would have no trouble believing him.

On Sunday 18 March 2001 Killie faced Celtic in the CIS Insurance League Cup final at Hampden, and held their own up until just before half-time, when Ian Durrant, the best player on the field, was forced to withdraw with injury, an injury from which he never really recovered and which eventually finished his playing career. Celtic's Henrik Larsson scored early in the second half, and from there on they dominated the game to run out comfortable 3-0 winners, with Larsson scoring all three goals.